DUPLIN
COUNTY
CEMETERY
RECORDS

VOLUME C

LEON H. SIKES

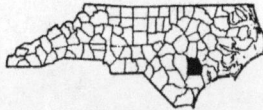

DUPLIN COUNTY HISTORICAL SOCIETY
ROSE HILL, NORTH CAROLINA
1986

Please direct all correspondence and orders to:

www.southernhistoricalpress.com
or
SOUTHERN HISTORICAL PRESS, Inc.
PO BOX 1267
375 West Broad Street
Greenville, SC   29601
southernhistoricalpress@gmail.com

ISBN #0-89308-595-2

CONTENTS

Introduction v

Individuals Born Prior to 1800 vii

Cemetery Records. . . . . 1 – 82

Appendix:

      Duplin County Map (complete) 83

      Duplin County Map (section I). 85

      Duplin County Map (section II) 87

      Duplin County Map (section III) 89

      Duplin County Map (section IV) 91

Index:

      Cemetery Index 93

      Index of Names. . . . . 95 – 108

INTRODUCTION

With the completion of this volume, most of the cemeteries in the northern half of Duplin County that have survived will be recorded. Also, a few cemeteries are included that were omitted from previous volumes. These are from areas scattered throughout the county.

The data was collected over a two year perion—the winter months of 1983/84 and 1984/85.

To make it easier for the user to locate a cemetery, maps of Duplin County are included with each cemetery plotted. There is a complete map of the county, which is then enlarged and divided into four parts: I,II, III,IV. Each cemetery is numbered and plotted on a map by its number. A particular cemetery can be located by the map coordinates given for each one. For example: Holmes Cemetery, No. 2, F-3. To locate this cemetery on a map, first find the map with the coordinates F-3, and in the F-3 sector will be the number 2, indicating the Holmes Cemetery. There is also a written location description at the beginning of each cemetery listing which will provide a more detailed, specific site location.

The North Carolina Department of Transportation, Duplin County Map 1982, was used with this volume. Secondary road numbers (SR) are used in the location descriptions. (Note: A recent renumbering of certain roads in the county has changed SR 1002, running northward from the Albertson community, to NC 903. This change has been made here, but would not show on other 1982 Duplin County road maps.)

Included in this volume for interest and easier reference, is an alphabetical listing of the individuals born prior to 1800. (Page vii).

The abreviation (MM), is used to indicate a mortuary marker. The initials that were found on a few footstones that did not have a headstone were recorded, but not indexed.

The user of this book must be aware that each name was indexed only once. The name could appear more than one time per page!

There are 140 cemeteries listed here and 2,083 entries in the name index. This is the ninth volume of gravestone/cemetery records collected and published for Duplin County. The first volume was published in 1960. With the execption of the Pine Crest Cemetery in Warsaw, and the Calypso Cemetery in Calypso, these nine volumes contain the majority of the cemeteries in the county that have survived and contain readable markers. The Pine Crest Cemetery and the Calypso Cemetery are located in a more or less protected environment, hopefully ensuring their survival, and will be recorded at a later date. Rockfish Memorial Cemetery and other newer perpetual care cemeteries will also be recorded later.

INDIVIDUALS BORN PRIOR TO 1800

Page

Archelous Branch. 78

Esther Branch 78

James Carr. 81

Ann Carroll 79

John Carroll. 79

Patrick Ezzell. 73

Diana Griffin Faison. 44

Henry Faison. 44

Elizabeth Outlaw Grady. 76

Henry Grady 76

John Grady. 58

Eliza Jane Hooks Hatch. 62

Elisha Herring. 39

Rachel Herring. 44

Holloway Hodges 16

Margaret Hurst. 74

William Hurst 74

Barbara Mallard 78

John Mallard. 78

Hannah Green McGowen. 57

Joseph McGowen. 57

Capt. James Outlaw. 28

Hester Pickett. 58

William Pickett 58

James T. Rhodes 16

Mary Rhodes 16

Rev. Samuel Stanford. 44

Jesse Swinson 43

Nancy Swinson 43

Harper Williams 82

Lamuel Williams 68

Charity Wright. 74

Eliza Wright. 51

James Wright. 74

John Beck Wright. .74

Thomas Wright 51

1. DAIL CEMETERY (F-3)
> Located on SR 1524, .1 mile north of the junction with SR 1500, on the east side of the road.

Sarah Jane Dail: 13 Sep 1835 – 27 Oct 1892

Ann Wiley, wife of Budd Dail: 10 Nov 1859 – 13 Apr 1931, Mother

Budd Dail: 5 Nov 1859 – 20 Nov 1917, Father

Grace Dail: 13 Jun 1888 – 4 Jul 1927

Winlson Dail: 24 Apr 1905 – 6 Jul 1927

Ira Randolph Summerlin: 2 May 1926 – 1 Dec 1980, MM

Hepsie Jones Summerlin: 12 Mar 1893 – 28 Dec 1963

Mary Thigpen, wife of Phillip Jones: 1843 – 1924

Infant dau. of Ira & Hepsie Summerlin: No dates

Ira Summerlin, Jr., son of Ira & Hepsie Summerlin: 22 Jan 1924 – 2 Dec 1924

Minnie M., dau. of Ira & Hepsie Summerlin: 9 Oct 1921 – 13 Aug 1923

Rodolph Summerlin, son of Ira & Minnie Summerlin: 7 Nov 1895 – 13 Oct 1914

Ira Summerlin: 15 Sep 1871 – 8 Jun 1953
> same stone

Minnie Carter: 4 Aug 1883 – 7 Jun 1914

Haywood Summerlin: 15 Jul 1846 – 31 Dec 1892

William M. Herring: July 1875 – 7 Jun 1935

Leacy Jones, wife of Howell Dail: 15 Sep 1865 – 23 Nov 1941

Howell Dail: 13 Jul 1859 – 27 Dec 1940

Mamie Howell: 21 Nov 1896 – 3 May 1935

Infant of Jonas & Griza Dail: B.&d. 15 Feb 1924

Infant son of Jonas & Griza Dail: B.&d. 1 Dec 1913

Jonas Dail: 1 Nov 1893 – 11 Oct 1967
> same stone

Sonnie J.: 4 Sep 1896 – 18 Nov 1976
> same stone

Grizza D.: 15 Apr 1893 – 26 Sep 1933

Robert Jackson Dail: 13 Dec 1943 – 9 Jul 1961

Twins, son & dau. of Marvin & Sallie Dail:

Iris Carol Dail: B.&d. 21 Jun 1946
> same stone

Coris Gerald Dail: B.&d. 21 Jun 1946

Faison Dail: 21 Apr 1886 - 20 Jun 1941, Father
    same stone
Della Frances Kornegay, His wife: 1 Feb 1895 - 2 Dec 1981, Mother

Della E. Dail, dau. of Faison & Della Dail: 6 Nov 1926 - 9 Dec 1926

Mary Francis Dail, dau. of Faison & Della Dail: 6 Nov 1927 - 24 Dec 1927

John Donald Dail, son of Faison & Della K. Dail: 14 Oct 1931 - 6 Feb 1951
      Killed in action in Korea with the United Nations Forces,
      PFC 21 INF, 24 INF Division, Korea 2 PH

Henry Oliver Dail, son of Faison & Della K. Dail: 23 Dec 1937 - 6 Feb 1963

Mary Whitman Dail: 12 Sep 1900 - 8 May 1954, Mother

Eugene Dail: 11 Nov 1938 - 28 Jul 1981, MM

Marable Dail: 11 Nov 1911 - 17 Jan 1940
    same stone
Mallie Taylor, His wife: 4 Oct 1917 - n.d.

Delia A., wife of Wilson Dail: 30 Aug 1881 - 9 Oct 1931

Wilson Dail: 7 Jul 1884 - 10 Apr 1937

Ann Dail, dau. of Wilson & Rosa D. Dail: 16 May 1935 - 1 Apr 1939

W.N. Jones: 29 Mar 1868 - 16 Apr 1940, Father
    same stone
Sarah Dail, His wife: 7 Nov 1872 - 15 Feb 1932, Mother

Tallins Dail: 14 Jun 1862 - 26 Nov 1929

Jonah Dail: 12 Aug 1879 - 20 Mar 1934

Lawrence Albert Dail, son of Sampson & Ellen Dail: 3 May 1925 - 12 Aug 1940

Sampson Dail: 18 Mar 1895 - 9 Apr 1956

Ellen Dail Bishop: 19 Jul 1906 - 22 Dec 1978

James Henry Bishop: 6 Feb 1905 - 19 May 1974

Mathie Buck Dail: 23 Apr 1921 - 26 Jul 1961
    same stone
Doris Robinson: 1 Aug 1927 - n.d.

G. Frank Outlaw: 10 Feb 1904 - n.d.
    same stone
Mettie J.: 26 Oct 1906 - 23 Mar 1971

2. HOLMES CEMETERY (F-3)
    Located on SR 1525, .5 mile east from the junction with SR 1524
    on the north side of the road.

Jim Davis: 28 Jun 1910 - 14 Feb 1969, Husband

Kattie Belle Davis: 10 Jul 1915 – 4 Aug 1968, Wife

Mittie Davis: 17 Sep 1882 – 11 Feb 1955

MM unreadable

Infant son of Ivey & Nora Summerlin : 16 Apr 1938

Ivey Summerlin: 30 May 1911 – 5 Feb 1975
      same stone
Nora L.: 1 Sep 1911 – n.d.

George D. Waters: 12 Feb 1902 – n.d.
      same stone
Clara Bell: 20 Sep 1907 – 10 Jun 1941

Mildred Waters, dau. of G.D. & Clara B. Waters: 11 Sep 1932 – 15 Sep 1933

Carey D. Waters, son of G.D. & Clara B. Waters: 27 Aug 1934 – 2 Jul 1935

Thad Rogers: 19 Dec 1870 – 9 Oct 1957
      same stone
Alphina Outlaw: 13 Apr 1878 – 22 Mar 1954

Callie Mae Rodgers, dau. of Thad & Alphina Rogers: 5 Dec 1921 – 9 Nov 1922

Paul Rodgers, son of Thad & Pina Rogers: 25 Dec 1915 – 4 Jun 1917

Carl Rodgers, son of Thad & Pina Rogers: 8 Oct 1919 – 30 Aug 1920

Henry James Taylor: 11 Dec 1894 – 10 Mar 1954
      same stone
Cammie Rogers: 7 Jun 1902 – 13 Oct 1976

Marion McDonald Price: 3 Jun 1945 – 8 Sep 1968

Mary Sue Holmes, wife of John Holmes: 12 Sep 1889 – 17 Mar 1961

John Holmes: 12 Feb 1877 – 30 Mar 1941

Hadie Lou Holmes, dau. of John & Mary Sue Holmes: 14 NOv 1928 – 10 May 1930

Beulah Holmes, dau. of John & Mary Holmes: 7 May 1913 – 12 Jun 1914

Callie Homes, dau. of John & Mary Holmes: 12 Dec 1917 – 3 Aug 1919

Milfred Ray Davis, son of Calvin & Daisey Davis: 8 Sep 1932 – 16 Jun 1934

Nancy W. Herring: 1848 – 13 Oct 1929

Rosy Singleton, dau. of A.J. & Daisey A. Singleton: 24 Aug 1917 – n.d.

Alsa James Singleton: 20 Nov 1871 – 10 May 1926

Daisy Singleton Davis: 10 Apr 1890 – 15 Nov 1960

Calvin Davis: 27 Sep 1890 – 25 Apr 1956, N.C. PVT Co. B, 322 INF, WWI

Leslie Outlaw: 5 May 1909 – 13 Oct 1958
    same stone
Emma: 6 Nov 1913 – n.d., Married 11 Nov 1935

Larry James Outlaw: 14 Nov 1945 – 8 Sep 1968

Infant son of J.C. & A.L. Thigpen: 27 Sep 1921

Infant twin son of B.H. & Lucy Outlaw: 13 Nov 1914 – 2 Dec 1914

Infant twin son of B.H. & Lucy Outlaw: 13 Nov 1914 – 2 Dec 1914

Annie E. Outlaw, dau. of B.H. & Lucy Outlaw: 2 Dec 1916 – 8 Mar 1918

Mordecai Outlaw: 15 Oct 1907 – 25 Dec 1975
    same stone
Viola H.: 10 Sep 1911 – n.d.

Lawton Outlaw: 21 Nov 1873 – 10 Dec 1960, Father
    same stone
Emma M.: 4 Dec 1882 – 29 Jan 1936, Mother

Selma Jane Outlaw, dau. of Lawton & Emma M. Outlaw: 7 Oct 1915 – 2 May 1

Alma Irene OUtlaw, dau. of Lawton & Emma M. Outlaw: 1 Feb 1918 – 22 Sep

Joseph Edward Outlaw, son of Lawton & Emma M. Outlaw: 6 May 1913 – 15 Ap

Edd G. Carter: 27 Apr 1902 – n.d. , Husband
    same stone
Fannie M. Carter: 3 Feb 1906 – 14 Nov 1949, Wife
    same stone
Alma B. Carter: 25 Nov 1909 – 4 Mar 1980

3. GRADY CEMETERY (F-2)
    Located on SR 1524, .6 mile NW of the junction with SR 1525,
    on the west side of the road.

J. Franklin Arnette: 17 Jun 1913 – 6 Aug 1942

MM unreadable

MM unreadable

Glennie W. Grady: 10 Sep 1877 – 29 Apr 1939
    same stone
Ira Albert Grady: 1 May 1876 – n.d.

4. SULLIVAN CEMETERY (E-2)
    Located on SR 1524, .1 mile east of the junction with SR 1507,
    on the north side of the road in a field.

Henry Sullivan: 24 Sep 1905 – 3 Jun 1970

George Washington Sullivan: 24 Sep 1905 – 30 Dec 1974

John Henry Sullivan: 3 Apr 1863 – 29 Oct 1918

Georgia Taylor Sullivan: 20 Jun 1876 – 3 Jun 1960

Hoyt Jackson Sullivan, son of H. & Georgia Sullivan: 28 Sep 1897 – 20 Jun 1901

John Henry Jones: 13 Feb 1864 – 26 Mar 1937

Susan Holmes: 15 May 1854 – 18 Mar 1928

5. LONG RIDGE FREE WILL BAPTIST CHURCH CEMETERY (F-3)
        Located on SR 1500, 1 mile west of Scotts Store crossroads
        on the north side of the road.

Benjamin Haywood Outlaw: 5 Jun 1876 – 29 Jan 1956
        same stone
Lucy Gallagher: 8 Jun 1876 – 30 Jan 1956

Jessie O. Thigpen: 22 May 1903 – n.d. , Mother
        same stone
Alex Thigpen: 26 Feb 1891 – 26 Aug 1981, Father

Elbert F. Kornegay: 3 Nov 1936 – 13 Aug 1967

Richard A. Kornegay: MM, n.d.

Daniel Richard Kornegay: 11 Feb 1911 – 26 Nov 1957
        same stone
Beulah Summerlin: 29 Sep 1914 – n.d.

Daniel Lee Kornegay: 6 Sep 1861 – 17 Jun 1952
        same stone
Rachel Jones: 28 Apr 1869 – 4 Nov 1957

Lewis Jones: 1866 – 1948
        same stone
Jennie: 1873 – 1953

Wilbert W. Price: 29 Oct 1910 – 22 Aug 1957
        same stone
Essie Mae: 9 Jul 1907 – n.d.

Daniel Roscoe Sutton: 4 Aug 1907 – 7 Apr 1971, Father

Infant son of Jessie & Nellie Sutton: 15 Oct 1956

Jessie Sutton: 7 Aug 1906 – 19 Apr 1976
        same stone
Nellie W. Sutton: 13 Jul 1922 – n.d.

Infant Angela D. Parrott: 19 Nov 1950

William E. Sutton: 18 Dec 1932 – 14 Dec 1950

Ben Sutton: 7 Dec 1900 – 13 May 1977, Father
    same stone
Pearl Wilkins: 28 Jun 1915 – n.d. , Mother

Leroy Holmes: 6 Sep 1932 – 16 Oct 1970
    same stone
Viola W. : 7 May 1935 – n.d.

Major Holmes : 1890 – 1957
    same stone
Betty : 1891 – n.d.

MM unreadable

Clayton F. Holmes : 14 Apr 1929 – 9 Apr 1962

6. McGOWEN CEMETERY (E-5)
    Located on SR 1378, .2 mile south of the junction with SR 1380
    on the east side of the road between poultry houses.

Margia S. Stokes McGowen, wife of James H. McGowen :
    26 Aug 1842 – 14 Nov 1909

[broken stone: _?_ _?_ 1835 – _?_ _?_ 1913]

7. HERRING CEMETERY (G-3)
    Located on SR 1501, .2 mile north of the junction with SR 1566,
    on the east side of the road in a field.

Maggie Emma Blanton, T.B. & C.R. Blanton: 19 May 1922 – 29 Oct 1941

Daniel R. Herring, son of Henry & Winnie E. Herring : 23 Jul 1937 – 25 J

Henry E. Herring, son of Henry & Winnie E. Herring :
    11 May 1935 – 19 Jun 1938

Sallie Earnesteen Williams, dau. of Lesley & Fannie Williams:
    27 Nov 1928 – 18 Feb 1929

Johnie Randal Herring, son of Henry & Inez Herring:
    21 Aug 1927 – 6 Sep 1927

Carrie Ineze, wife of Henry Herring: 14 Apr 1907 – 28 Jul 1928

Henry Herring: 1 Jun 1904 – 20 Jan 1956, Father
    same stone
Winnie : 12 Sep 1913 – n.d. , Mother

Daniel Herring Jr. : 27 Mar 1882 – 22 Jan 1936

Daniel Herring :   25 Sep 1855 - 8 Apr 1926

Della, wife of Daniel Herring: 3 Oct 1875 - 11 Jul 1929

Fred Herring : 2 Dec 1897 - 20 Nov 1968, Father
    same stone
Pearl P. : 9 Jun 1907 - n.d. , Mother, Married 31 Jul 1924

Clifton H. Herring, son of Fred & Pearl Herring : 19 May 1939 - 1 Mar 1965

8. KORNEGAY CEMETERY (G-3)
       Located on SR 1501, .2 mile north of the junction with SR 1519,
       on the west side of the road.

Infant son of J.F. & Zilphia Kornegay: 9 Dec 1905 - 20 Dec 1905

Joseph F. Kornegay : 16 Jan 1854 - 4 Dec 1914

Zilphia F. Smith Kornegay, wife of J. Fisher Kornegay :
    3 Mar 1870 - 6 Nov 1955

Matthew J. Kornegay : 19 Sep 1885 - 5 Apr 1945

9. KORNEGAY CEMETERY (G-3)
       Located on SR 1501, .3 mile south of the intersection with SR 1519,
       on the east side of road, .2 mile up a dirt path.

Infant dau. of W.R. & Ollie Kornegay : 24 Sep 1954

Nick Kornegay : 14 FEb 1899 - 16 Nov 1933

N.D. Kornegay : 16 Aug 1862 - 17 Nov 1933

Alice Kornegay, wife of N.D. Kornegay : 4 Sep 1862 - 11 Feb 1904

Infant son of Wooten & Arrie Kornegay : [no dates]

Harvey Kornegay, son of Wooten & Arrie Kornegay : 7 Mar 1901 - 14 Oct 1901

Virginia Herring, wife of Daniel Herring: 3 May 1858 - 15 Jan 1895

Mary E., wife of George Daily : 7 May 1849 - 2 Mar 1930

Delphia E. Herring, dau. of Jeff & Connie S. Herring:
    15 Aug 1919 - 14 Dec 1919

Laura Kornegay, dau. of J.D. & A.E. Kornegay : 31 Aug 1895 - 28 Jul 1928

J.D. Kornegay : 14 Dec 1855 - 12 Dec 1921

Annie E., wife of J.D. Kornegay : 1 Jul 1860 - 7 Apr 1911

Martha J., wife of Daniel Kornegay : 13 Dec 1828 – 25 May 1904

Daniel Kornegay : 25 Dec 1819 – 28 Feb 1894

Arrie, wife of Wooten Kornegay : 2 Jul 1871 – 27 Feb 1913

Wooten Kornegay : 21 Feb 1870 – 4 May 1930
      same stone
Lola E. Smith, wife of Wooten Kornegay : 1 Mar 1880 – 28 Dec 1941

Thomas J. Kornegay : 6 Jul 1864 – 9 Oct 1930
      same stone
Alice Daly : 19 Sep 1873 – 28 Feb 1934

Arthur Randal Kornegay : 31 Oct 1909 – 25 Aug 1940

Arthur Kornegay : 18 Oct 1882 – 12 Dec 1930

Elizabeth K. Kornegay : 17 Sep 1882 – 3 Dec 1954

Keneth Ray Smith : 3 Jan 1936 – 28 Feb 1937

Infant of Willie & Maggie Smith : b. & d. 13 Apr 1933

Margret May Smith, dau. of Willie & Maggie Smith : 23 Jul 1930 – 19 Oct

Willie Smith : 5 Mar 1900 – 15 Dec 1936

Maggie K. Smith, wife of Chancy I. Smith : 19 Jun 1903 – 18 Oct 1970

Chancey Ivey Smith : 30 Jan 1908 – 24 Apr 1978

Evelyn W. Kornegay, dau. of George R. & Annie Kornegay :
      3 Sep 1920 – 10 Feb 1922

Randolph Kornegay, son of Duff & Louise Kornegay: 4 Dec 1924 – 2 Feb 192

10. TAYLOR CEMETERY (F-2)
      Located on SR 1523, .2 mile west from the junction with SR 1502,
      on the south side of the road.

Gurney Taylor : 1 Aug 1911 – 23 Apr 1970

Paul Taylor : 26 Oct 1914 – 8 Nov 1972

Budd Taylor : 11 Feb 1886 – 4 Jan 1958
      same stone
Polly : 1 May 1888 – 28 Dec 1962

James Taylor : 16 Sep 1919 – 6 Feb 1920

Baby Taylor : 29 Nov 1926 – 18 Dec 1926

Infant son of Will & Carrie Taylor : 17 Feb 1936

James R. Taylor :   1864 – 1920
    same stone
Beadie Taylor :   1867 – 1937

Mrs. Coreen Hill Alphin :   27 Jul 1923 – 1 Mar 1981, MM

MM unreadable

Ben Frank Taylor, son of Ben & Mattie Taylor: 2 Oct 1923 – 21 Nov 1923

Infant son of Ben & Mattie Taylor :   19 Jun 1931

Infant son of Ben & Mattie Taylor :   16 Jul 1935

Infant son of Ben & Mattie Taylor :   7 May 1939

Ben Taylor :   16 Sep 1900 – 22 Mar 1972
    same stone
Mattie Taylor :   1 Jul 1905 – n.d.

11. BENNETT CEMETERY (F-2)
    Located on SR 1502, .7 mile north of the intersection with SR 1501,
    (Blizzards Crossroads), on the east side of the road.

MM unreadable

MM unreadable

Benjamin Frank Bennett : 1861 – 1929
    same stone
John Anna Taylor Bennett :   1880 – 1938

MM unreadable

Willie Clifton Lamm :   27 May 1925 – 25 Nov 1925

Joseph J. Buchan :   11 Nov 1869 – 13 Dec 1941

Lillie, wife of J.J. Buchan :   30 Sep 1884 – 18 Jun 1913

Earl Buchan, son of J.J. & Lillie Buchan :   6 Dec 1903 – 6 Jan 1904

Infant of William R. & Mary L. Barwick : [no dates]

John Holland, Corp. Co. H, 66 NC INF, CSA

Geo. D. Quinn :   17 Oct 1882 – 22 Sep 1933

Daniel R. Bennett :   7 Nov 1859 – 31 May 1929
    same stone
Laura H. :   20 Aug 1865 – 8 Nov 1940

Jimmy D. Bennett :   6 Oct 1951 – 13 Jun 1973

Currie D. Bennett : 13 Dec 1917 – 20 Jan 1971
    NC Tec 5, 254 SIG HV CONST Co., WW II

Harold F. Bennett : 24 Sep 1926 – 22 Sep 1969

Albert S. Bennett : 16 Jun 1919 – 2 Dec 1965
    NC Tec 5, BTRY A, 545 FIELD ART, WW II

Eula Bennett : 17 Jun 1910 – 9 Mar 1967

Albert Bennett : 9 Sep 1892 – 21 Aug 1937, Husband & Daddy

Bertha J. Waters Bennett, wife of Albert Bennett :
    29 Dec 1892 – 3 May 1924, Sister

12. HERRING CEMETERY (F-2)
        Located on SR 1501, .5 east of the intersection with SR 1502,
        (Blizzards Crossroads), on the north side of the road.

George Glanton Herring : 4 Jul 1928 – 1 Feb 1968, PFC, US Army
    same stone
Marian Hardy Herring : 18 Dec 1938 – n.d.

Lannie Herring : 27 Sep 1893 – 11 Feb 1948, Father
    same stone
Lizzie : 5 Oct 1903 – 5 Nov 1955, Mother

Infant Herring : [no dates]

MM unreadable

Herbert Dail : 23 Dec 1890 – 16 Jun 1925

MM unreadable

Julia Herring : 10 Nov 1862 – 18 Dec 1945, Mother

Gid Herring : 12 Jul 1885 – 23 Nov 1945, Brother

Delia Herring : 19 Aug 1905 – 8 Jan 1967

Simpson Herring : Died 24 Jan 1942, Aged 70 years

Park Herring : 10 Oct 1913 – 12 May 1935

Laney Herring : 25 Apr 1873 – 3 Aug 1946

Needham Herring : 17 Oct 1863 – 25 May 1928

Charity E. Herring : 7 Sep 1885 – 20 Jan 1955

Fannie Herring : July 1856 – 10 Jun 1922, Mother

MM unreadable

Wooden marker unreadable

Jim Summerlin : 9 Apr 1860 – 25 May 1912

Mack Summerlin : Feb 1880 – 8 Jun 1938
    same stone
Bessie : 6 Jun 1910 – 13 Feb 1935

Robert Alphin : 21 Aug 1908 – 21 Aug 1965
    same stone
Ancie Taylor : 15 Dec 1912 – n.d.

Mary E. Alphin : 4 Aug 1869 – 23 Apr 1940

John Tarnce Alphin : 18 Aug 1889 – 14 Mar 1961

Victoria Turner Alphin : 3 Dec 1897 – 14 Sep 1953

Garland O. Alphin, infant son of Tarnce & Victoria Alphin :
    b. & d. 1920

Annie G., wife of David Goodman : 3 Jan 1861 – 28 Jul 1915, Mother

Katie Lucile Alphin, dau. of Mr. & Mrs. J.D. Alphin :
    6 Aug 1927 – 26 Dec 1923

MM unreadable

Rebecca Alphin : 13 Oct 1968

James Perry Turner : 17 Aug 1924 – 8 Jun 1982
    same stone
Esther Mae T. : 4 Jan 1922 – 1 May 1980

Alfred Turner : 10 Aug 1900 – 12 Nov 1962
    same stone
Eva : 22 Jan 1904 – 5 Apr 1977

Effie Summerlin : 13 Sep 1886 – 8 Jun 1966

Norman Summerlin : 30 Nov 1920 – 12 Apr 1947

Garland Odell Turner : 2 Mar 1930 – 22 Dec 1968, NC PFC US Army

Yancey Alphin : 18 May 1918 – 18 Apr 1970, NC PFC BTRY D 400 AAA AW BN CAC WWII

13. JONES CEMETERY (G-3)
    Located on SR 1501, .8 mile N. of the junction with SR 1566, W. side of road

Ashley Jones : 28 Apr 1918 – 8 May 1974
    same stone
Callie Grady Jones : 9 Jan 1923 – n.d.

MM unreadable

Lula Mae C. Howard : 3 May 1929 – 11 Mar 1967

[Four MM unreadable]

John M. Summerlin : 6 Feb 1870 – 2 Jul 1943
      same stone
Eliza E. : 8 Sep 1873 –1 Jan ?

Sallie E. Summerlin, dau. of J.M. & Eliza Summerlin :
      11 Jun 1902 – 4 Jun 1904

Pearcy Jane Taylor : 19 Mar 1859 – 12 Dec 1942

[Four Wooden markers, unreadable]

Susan A. Jones : 1860 – 28 Feb 1927

14. WHITMAN CEMETERY (G-4)
      Located on SR 1514, .9 mile west from the junction with SR SR 1500,
      on the north side of the road, up a dirt path.

Lucille W. Grady : 6 Aug 1910 – 9 Dec 1950

George H. Whitman : 17 May 1872 – 26 Jul 1935
      same stone
Nora E., his wife : 14 Mar 1889 – 20 Apr 1968

Leon A. Outlaw : 25 Jun 1904 – 16 Sep 1970
      same stone
Beulah W. : 10 Jul 1907 – n.d.

Infant son of G.H. & Nora Whitman : 1915 [No other date]

15. WHITMAN CEMETERY (G-4)
      Located on SR 1514, 1.2 miles west of the junction with SR 1500,
      on the north side of the road, .2 mile in a field.

Betsey, wife of Riley Whitman : 12 Apr 1828 – 18 Dec 1903

MM unreadable

16. ROBERTS CEMETERY (D-3)
      Located on SR 1306, at the junction with SR 1363 on the south
      side of the road.

Alton Joyner : 15 May 1913 – 30 Nov 1960

Calhoun H. Joyner : 30 Sep 1880 – 5 Mar 1954

Sallie G. Joyner : 19 Feb 1887 – 6 Mar 1954

Nancy Katherine Roberts : 9 Aug 1891 – 30 Dec 1938

Bertice Carl Roberts, Sr. : 1 Sep 1897 – 15 Jul 1977

Infant dau. of B.C. & Annie Roberts : 10 Aug 1948

Robert W. Royall : 26 Aug 1934 – 10 Dec 1955

Arthur P. Royall : 16 Mar 1900 – 4 Sep 1945

Elizabeth Roberts Royall, wife of A.P. Royall : 19 Dec 1912 – 19 Jan 1938

Infant dau. of A.P. & Elizabeth Royall : 15 Jan 1938

Infant dau. of Ned & Margaret Roberts : 14 Sep 1928

Ned Roberts : 12 Feb 1905 – 22 May 1970

Jesse J. Quinn : 25 Jan 1893 – 13 Feb 1951

Mary R. Quinn : 6 May 1908 – 14 May 1980

Henry Roberts : 15 Mar 1871 – 18 Aug 1951

Melissa West, wife of Henry Roberts : 24 Nov 1872 – 24 Jan 1938

Jerry Lee Roberts : 1 Nov 1927 – 16 May 1928

Richard O. Ward : 3 Mar 1937 – 12 Sep 1966

17. BROCK CEMETERY (C-2)
      Located on SR 1306, .1 mile north of the junction with SR 1316,
      on the east side of the road.

Sallie Leona Brock : 8 Oct 1910 – 26 Sep 1945

Henry Herman Brock : 27 Oct 1904 – 20 Aug 1963

Infant son of Mallie & Henry Brock : 10 Feb 1955 – 11 Feb 1955

James A. Swinson : 13 Apr 1890 – 16 Apr 1956
      same stone
Rossie W. : 9 Jul 1890 – 3 Jun 1965

Betty Gale Swinson, dau. of Bobby S. & JoAnn Swinson :
      27 Dec 1959 – 8 Mar 1960

[The following were in a separate fence adjoining the previous cemetery]

Larry Joe Pate : 1 Oct 1947 – 12 Dec 1966

Carlyle Franklin Pate : 23 Aug 1913 – 26 Jul 1975
    same stone
Ruby Lee Brogden : 2 Oct 1916 – n.d., Married 29 Dec 1935

18. UNDERHILL CEMETERY (G-1)
    Located on SR 1559, .6 mile west of the junction with SR 1558,
    on the north side of the road, .3 mile in a field.

William Henry Bowden, son of B.N. & S.E. Bowden :
    12 Jan 1895 – 12 Jul 1920

Levia B. Bowden, son of B.N. & S. Bowden : 25 Mar 1902 – 11 Jul 1903

Annie F. Underhill, dau. of G.W. & Littie A. Underhill :
    18 May 1922 – 23 May 1922
    same stone
Frances Underhill : 14 May 1849 – 7 Dec 1908, Mother
    same stone
George W. Underhill : 4 Jul 1889 – 28 Jun 1937

J.W. Underhill : 4 Mar 1849 – 23 Oct 1922, Father

[There were several other unmarked graves here]

19. DICKSON CEMETERY (B-2)
    Located on NC 403, .2 mile east from the junction with SR 1320,
    on the north side of the road on a hill in a field.

*Anne Eliza Dickson : 4 Jan 1839 – 30 Jul 1861

Ann Clopton Dickson : 13 Apr 1813 – 12 Aug 1862

Dr. James G. Dickson : 26 Aug 1809 – *8 Sep 1867

Sallie Jane Dickson, wife of Dr. James G. Dickson :
    2 Oct 1829 – 16 Aug 1913

Joseph L. Dickson : 27 Jul 1865 – 15 Jan 1928

Sallie J. Dickson, wife of Joseph L. Dickson : 1 Feb 1867 – 15 Aug 1908

  ?   Dixon : 10 Jan 1903 – 12 Feb 1903 [stone broken]

*From the records of Mrs. H.B. Kornegay, Sr.,
  recorded in 1968.

20. BOWDEN-BROADHURST CEMETERY (B-1)
    Located on SR 1373, .4 mile east from the junction with SR 1318,
    on the north side of the road.

Lee C. Cherry : 7 Jun 1877 - 3 Mar 1906

Eliza L. Cherry, wife of L.F. Barnes, mother of L.T. Barnes :
    9 May 1835 - 17 Aug 1910

Jim W. Dixon : 17 Nov 1851 - 27 Feb 1928

Polly L., wife of J.D. Thornton : 25 Mar 1879 - 29 Mar 1911

Wellie E. Dixon, son of James W. & Mary J. Dixon :
    5 Feb 1892 - 20 Jul 1902

Mary J. Dixon, wife of James W. Dixon : 22 May 1857 - 26 Jul 1896

Johnnie M.A. Herring, infant son of John L. & Emma Herring :
    28 May 1889 - 13 Aug 1889

Emma Herring, wife of John L. Herring : 14 Mar 1862 - 28 May 1889

W.S. Bowden : 20 Aug 1820 - 23 Jul 1906, Father

Annie J. Bowden, wife of W.S. Bowden : 22 Jan 1815 - 4 Nov 1888

Clyde Lewis Broadhurst : 3 Apr 1888 - 28 Dec 1969
    same stone
Allen Manley Broadhurst : 19 Jul 1882 - 14 Jul 1951

Bryant W. Cherry : 24 Dec 1848 - 12 Dec 1912
    same stone
Julia A. : 22 Nov 1858 - 2 Jul 1929

John Broadhurst : 8 Jun 1847 - 3 Jan 1921, Father
    same stone
Helen C. : 11 Mar 1858 - 30 Jan 1925, Mother

[Small stone, unreadable]

Ernest C. Bowden, son of S.A. & Penina Bowden : 28 Apr 1886 - 30 Dec 1896

Samuel Allen Bowden : 3 Apr 1858 - 20 Dec 1928
    same stone
Penina Cameron : 28 Jun 1859 - 24 Dec 1928

M.W. Sutton : 18 Nov 1864 - 30 Apr 1900

Ida L. Sutton : 18 Mar 1871 - 4 Nov 1904, Mother

John Allen Broadhurst : 10 Jul 1912 - 17 Mar 1940

21. RHODES CEMETERY (B-3)
    Located on SR 1304, 1.2 miles south of the junction with SR 1322,
    on the west side of the road, .3 mile in a field.

[All the names were on one monument]

John F. Rhodes : [no dates]

James T. Rhodes : Died 3 Oct 1834, Age 61-8

Mary Rhodes, wife of James T. Rhodes : Died 9 Oct 1834, Age 52-6-15

Ann Rhodes : Died 17 Aug 1848, Age 43-5-10

Mary Rhodes : Died 26 Aug 1844, Age 34-6-12

Temperance Rhodes : Died 27 Mar 1831, Age 24-0-2

Rachel Rhodes : Died 1818, Age 4 years

Maria Rhodes : Died 1820, Age 6 months

Joseph T. Rhodes : [no dates]

Maria S. Rhodes, wife of Joseph T. Rhodes : Died 4 Apr 1844, Age 27-6-13

Mary P. Rhodes : Died 31 Jan 1840, Age 3-10-3

Martha R. Shine : Died 8 Aug 1841, Age 4-4-19

[This last one was on a separate marker]
Elizabeth Shine, wife of James F. Shine : Died 25 Sep 1857, in her 38th yea

22. HODGES CEMETERY (B-3)
    Located on SR 1304, 1 mile south of the junction with SR 1322,
    .3 mile off the road on the east side, in a field.

Holloway Hodges : Died 3 Jan 1819, Age 60 years

C.S. [on a footstone]

23. MILLER CEMETERY (C-3)
    Located on SR 1304, .5 mile south of the junction with SR 1354,
    .1 mile off the road on the east side.

Clara Miller : 20 Jun 1888 - 11 Oct 1963

Mary C. Miller : 28 Jul 1884 - 16 Nov 1968

Annie E. Miller, wife of W.J. Miller : 12 Jun 1849 - 13 Oct 1915

William James Miller : 17 Mar 1847 - 29 Dec 1913

Lonnie Daniel Miller : 18 Sep 1886 - 20 Jan 1943

Charlie William Miller : 12 Aug 1920 - 31 Oct 1920
     same stone
Lonnie D. Miller : 27 Dec 1930 - 15 May 1931
     same stone
Eliza Mae Miller : 13 Sep 1932 - 3 May 1933
 "Children of W.B. & Elizabeth T. Miller" [On the bottom of the marker]

Ora Ozzella Miller : 8 May 1908 - 25 Dec 1929

Margaret A. Miller : 25 Jan 1871 - 25 Aug 1940

J.R. Miller : 12 Jul 1872 - 25 Aug 1922

Bethania J. Miller : 11 Apr 1904 - 30 Mar 1947

Hez L. Miller : 29 May 1882 - 29 Aug 1935, Father

William Loyd Miller : 1905 - 1967, Husband

24. SWINSON CEMETERY (C-3)
     Located on SR 1305, .1 mile north of the junction with SR 1358,
     .5 mile off the road on the south side on a farm road.

Christopher C. James : 22 Nov 1830 - 26 May 1893

Mary S. Swinson, wife of Christopher C. James :
     6 Sep 1839 - 14 Dec 1906

John P. James : 24 Dec 1860 - 12 May 1944

Obedience Joyner, wife of John P. James : 16 Feb 1874 - 7 Oct 1935

Jesse Swinson : 8 Jan 1830 - 26 Dec 1909
     same stone
Alice Roosevelt Swinson : 6 Jun 1902 - 2 Feb 1912
     same stone
George Marcus Swinson : 30 Oct 1887 - 8 Nov 1912
 "Children of Jesse & Lola Swinson" [On the bottom of marker]
     same stone
Cyrus Thompson Swinson : 22 May 1892 - 4 Nov 1899
     same stone
Gurtrude Swinson : 7 Jul 1896 - 29 Dec 1911
 "Children of Jesse & Lola Swinson" [On bottom of marker]

Henry Swinson, son of Daniel & Charlotte Swinson :
     6 Sep 1817 - 27 Jun 1854

Henry K. Bailey, son of J.F. & M.F. Bailey : 4 Nov 1885 - 18 Sep 1886

Charlie H. Swinson :   31 Aug 1878 - 11 Jun 1949

Callie Brock, wife of C.H. Swinson :   8 Sep 1890 - 6 Jan 1934

Joe Swinson :   15 Oct 1888 - 10 Dec 1943
     same stone
Myrtle Ann Jones :   22 Nov 1891 - n.d.

Andrew T. Swinson, husband of Mary E. Swinson :
     22 Jul 1835 - 1 Apr 1904

Mary E. Hardy, wife of Andrew T. Swinson :
     21 Mar 1847 - 2 May 1935

Margarette Lee Swinson, dau. of Ben & Minnie Swinson :
     20 Aug 1915 - 30 Jul 1919

Susan, wife of John Swinson :   1803 - 30 Aug 1854

Frances W. Swinson, dau. of John & Susan Swinson : 9 Sep 1821 - 7 May 1853
     [There were many other unmarked graves here]

25. SUMMERLIN CEMETERY (E-3)
     Located on SR 1306, on the NE corner of the intersection of SR 1004
     and SR 1306, (Summerlins Crossroads).

James Clifton Outlaw :   27 Sep 1927 - 27 Mar 1953

Cleveland Outlaw :   29 Sep 1884 - 30 Jan 1963, Father
     same stone
Dora Blizzard :   1 Sep 1887 - 29 Sep 1950, Mother

Twin infants of Luke & Julia Rogers :   25 Oct 1928

George Rodgers, son of Chancey & Georgia Rodgers :   Age 8 years, [no date]

Lula Rodgers, dau. of Chancey & Georgia Rodgers :   Age 4 years, [no date]

Chancey Rodgers :   17 Apr 1869 - 11 Oct 1943
     same stone
Georgiana :   29 Oct 1868 - n.d.

Eula L. Lamb :   27 Jul 1892 - 26 Aug 1912

Henrettia Summerlin, wife of F.C. Outlaw : 13 Nov 1862 - 16 Feb 1923

F.C. Outlaw :   13 Nov 1861 - 17 Jul 1928

Floyd Summerlin, son of John Daniel & Zilphia Ann Summerlin :
     2 Jan 1871 - 12 Nov 1873

Alonzo Daniel Summerlin, son of John Daniel & Zilphia Ann Summerlin :
22 Feb 1879 - 2 Jun 1892

Leon ?   Outlaw, Jr. : Died 29 Nov 1974, Age 50 years, MM

MM unreadable

Leon D. Outlaw : 8 Feb 1892 - 3 Sep 1948
same stone
Decie H. : 8 Jul 1894 - 29 Oct 1961

Herman Outlaw : 1914 - 1917

Infant dau. of G.E. & F.V. Alphin : 7 Oct 1892 - 11 Oct 1892

Florence, wife of G.E. Alphin : 22 Nov 1865 - 22 Nov 1892

Zilphia Ann, wife of John Daniel Summerlin : 21 Sep 1844 - 5 Sep 1888

John D. Summerlin : 9 Apr 1833 - 23 Jun 1912

Benjamin P. Summerlin : 15 Jan 1876 - 12 Aug 1948 [Masonic emblem]
same stone
Maggie K. : 31 Aug 1884 - 31 Jan 1943

Samuel Paul Summerlin, son of J.L. & Margaret Summerlin :
21 Oct 1928 - 19 Feb 1937

Margaret Parker, wife of J.L. Summerlin : 18 Jul 1903 - 8 Mar 1966

James Earl Grady, Sr. : 23 Sep 1912 - n.d.
same stone
Mildred Kelly Summerlin, wife of James E. Grady, Sr. :
4 Oct 1915 - 28 Jul 1971

Walter Lee Hinson : 28 Sep 1902 - 6 Jul 1968
same stone
Hazel Summerlin : 3 Jul 1915 - n.d.

Robert Lee Summerlin : 1 Aug 1877 - 19 Dec 1949
same stone
Cornelia Kilpatrick Summerlin Jernigan : 12 Apr 1899 - 3 Jun 1980
same stone
Ada J. Summerlin : 25 Jun 1884 - 22 Mar 1920

Infant [stone buried]

T.A. Jernigan : 23 Dec 1881 - 21 May 1967
same stone
Annie D. Summerlin, wife of T.A. Jernigan : 9 Feb 1883 - 22 Nov 1951

John Allen Jernigan, son of Annie & Allen Jernigan : 15 Jan 1911 - 23 Jan1912

Thurman Allen Jernigan : 18 NOv 1914 - 10 Nov 1964
same stone
Rosedene Sloan : 7 Dec 1916 - n.d.

Samuel C. Cherry : 15 Dec 1907 - 16 Jun 1966
    same stone
Gertrude : 16 Oct 1913 - n.d.

Hannah Harrette, wife of Sampson Pierce : 1 Sep 1837 - 15 Feb 1917

Sampson Pierce : 4 Jul 1838 - 7 Dec 1917

Nancy Susan Pierce : 1876 - 1954

Annie B. Howard, dau. of J.W. & Bettie Howard : 11 Sep 1920 - 30 Sep 1920

W.C. Summerlin : 25 Mar 1873 - 29 Jan 1925, Father
    same stone
Minnie W. : 29 Mar 1878 - 4 Mar 1974, Mother

McCoy Stephen Summerlin : 23 Feb 1915 - 2 Oct 1973
    same stone
Nannie Lou Grady : 27 Jun 1914 - n.d.

Addie Summerlin, wife of Robert T. Potter : 18 Jan 1888 - 15 Jul 1956

Robert C. Potter : 16 Nov 1911 - 1 Jul 1969

Paul Potter : 18 Dec 1919 - 2 Oct 1979

James K. Alexander : 9 Jan 1894 - 6 Feb 1978
    same stone
Rovenia P. : 7 May 1907 - n.d., Married 3 Apr 1929

George Lawton Summerlin : 22 Oct 1881 - 6 Apr 1957
    same stone
Kate Agnes Williams, wife of George Lawton Summerlin :
    8 Sep 1892 - 26 Apr 1968

Infant son of G.L. & Kate Summerlin : 9 Jun 1928

Walter Jones : 12 Nov 1903 - 20 Aug 1976
    same stone
Mabel W. : 20 Nov 1908 - n.d.

Mary Ann Outlaw, dau. of Mr. & Mrs. Lester Outlaw : 9 Aug 1957 - 16 Apr 196

Johnnie W. Outlaw : 1896 - 1967, Father
    same stone
Trudie M. : 1898 - 1964, Mother

Robert L. Rogers : 29 Feb 1912 - 2 Nov 1973
    same stone
Ruth O. : 25 Sep 1920 - n.d.

Infant son of Mr. & Mrs. Herman Quinn : 11 Oct 1941

Arthur Outlaw :   28 Oct 1889 - 14 Jul 1945
     same stone
Martha Harrell, wife of Arthur Outlaw :   23 Apr 1891 - 14 May 1981

26. PARKER CEMETERY (D-3)
     Located on SR 1004, .3 mile north of the junction with SR 1505,
     on the east side of the road.

Mathew Parker : 13 Jul 1885 - 11 May 1961, Husband
     same stone
Sula : 3 Jan 1887 - 19 Nov 1963, Wife

Senas Parker : 1848 - 1888
     same stone
Celia, his wife : 1860 - 1923,"Parents of Mathew & Berry Parker"

Infant [no dates]

Joe Berry Parker : 9 Oct 1886 - 23 Feb 1935
     same stone
Annie Garner : 24 Mar 1896 - 8 Feb 1971

27. OUTLAW CEMETERY (D-3)
     Located on SR 1004, .1 mile south of the junction with SR 1504,
     on the west side of the road.

Ray L. Outlaw : 27 Jun 1923 - 10 Mar 1948, NC TEC 5 331 ORD DEPOT CO, WWII

Willie I. Outlaw : 29 Nov 1879 - 2 Mar 1942, NC CPL CO. C 15 REGT INF
     same stone
Nettie Herring : 22 Jul 1887 - 17 May 1961

Andrew J. Outlaw : 29 Nov 1915 - 28 Oct 1963, NC TEC 4 CO. H 36 ARMD REGT WWII
     same stone
Lucille Jones : 10 Jun 1927 - n.d.

28. OUTLAW CEMETERY (D-2)
     Located on SR 1004, .4 mile north of the junction with SR 1504,
     on the west side of the road.

Anna Davis, wife of D.W. Williams : 26 Jun 1851 - 8 Dec 1919

D.W. Williams : 30 Jun 1843 - 16 Jun 1924

Holand W. Outlaw : 12 Jul 1912 - 28 Jun 1983, MM

Laure Heath, wife of J.J. Outlaw : 16 Mar 1887 - 30 Jul 1922

MM unreadable

Norman Deleon Outlaw :   27 May 1909 – 6 Aug 1983
    same stone
Bessie C. :   29 Aug 1909 – 25 May 1935

D.J. Outlaw :   17 Jul 1845 – 26 Sep 1916

Clarence Outlaw, son of D.J. Outlaw :   1 Apr 1885 – 8 Dec 1889

J.W. Outlaw, Sr. :   17 Sep 1850 – 27 Feb 1919, Father
    same stone
Susan A. Summerlin, His wife :   31 Aug 1855 – 18 Nov 1903, Mother

William L. Outlaw, son of Hettie & Samuel Outlaw :
    23 Sep 1921 – 27 Dec 1922

Samuel Outlaw :   23 Sep 1890 – 23 Aug 1924

Infant son of Joe & Emma Outlaw :   28 Jun 1917

Joseph Outlaw :   22 Aug 1887 – 26 Jun 1938

Emma D. Outlaw :   6 Jul 1888 – 7 Oct 1975

Charlie D. Outlaw :   29 Oct 1881 – 7 Nov 1946
      same stone
Ella Heath :   12 Mar 1891 – 25 Dec 1976

29. WINDERS CEMETERY (D-2)
    Located on SR 1363, .5 mile west of the junction with SR 1004,
    on the south side of the road.

Infant son of Edward & Martha Ghlighen : Died 23 Sep 1862, [no age]

Walter Lee Winders, son of Luther & Sarah Winders :
    5 Nov 1880 – 16 Dec 1883

John R. Southerland :   20 May 1854 – 15 Jul 1917
    same stone
Sophronie Winders, his wife :   23 Jan 1857 – 29 Jan 1931

Mrs. Ruby [Pearl?] Southerland : Died Jan 1975, Age 63 years, MM

Leonard G. Southerland :   16 May 1878 – 6 Apr 1946
    same stone
Cannie E. Grady, his wife : 3 Jul 1879 – 29 Aug 1963
    same stone
Flora Bell Southerland, their dau. :   27 Nov 1909 – 6 Dec 1954

Ruby P. Southerland :   19 Sep 1911 – 4 Jan 1975

Infant son of L.G. & C.E. Southerland :24 Feb 1917 – 25 Feb 1917

Infant dau. of L.G. & C.E. Southerland : 2 Feb 1916 – 7 Feb 1916

Ruth Mildred Southerland, dau. of C.C. & Annie M. Southerland :
7 Nov 1914 - 8 Jan 1916

Charles Clay Southerland : 7 Apr 1885 - 13 Jul 1938, Father
same stone
Annie Best : 1 Jan 1895 - 7 Nov 1964, Mother

Infant son of Henry & Ren V. Southerland : 15 Jul 1928

Cecil Garland Southerland, son of H.D. & Wren Southerland :
5 Aug 1930 - 14 Mar 1935

Abbie W., wife of E.B. Southerland : 8 Jan 1886 - 27 Dec 1914

30. BROCK CEMETERY (D-3)
Located on SR 1363, .6 mile north of the junction with SR 1362,
on the east side of the road.

Leslie Ray Brock : 26 Oct 1926 - 1 Jul 1943

Betty Lynn White : 31 May 1964 - 1 Jun 1964

Charlie G. Kennedy, son of C.G. & Essie Kennedy :
22 May 1926 - 3 Dec 1930

Charlie G. Kennedy : 23 Aug 1898 - 1 Apr 1970
same stone
Essie B. : 5 Jun 1896 - 19 Apr 1981

George W. Miller : 13 Sep 1882 - 27 Oct 1949, Father

Lela B. Miller : 26 Feb 1895 - 25 Dec 1961, Mother

John A. Page : 9 May 1852 - 7 Oct 1921

MM unreadable

MM unreadable

Infant son of Mr. & Mrs. Frederick Storaska : b. & d. 15 Mar 1969

Charlie M. Nicholson : 7 Mar 1897 - 31 Dec 1963, Father
same stone
Georgia B. : 30 Mar 1892 - 10 Nov 1969, Mother, Married 8 Feb 1915

Minnie Lee Brock : 22 Apr 1890 - 7 Feb 1891

Infant dau. [no other data]

Francenia, wife of Mack Brock : 19 May 1861 - 21 Mar 1941

Mack Brock : 17 May 1855 - 13 Apr 1923

Kater Morris Nicholson : 1 Oct 1920 - 27 Apr 1953,
   NC TEC 4 47 ENGINEER C BN WWII

George D. Eatmon :   29 Oct 1935 - 30 Jun 1983

Robert E. Eatmon, Jr. :   26 Dec 1926 - 17 Jun 1928

George W. Brock :   9 Jan 1849 - 30 Aug 1921, Father
   same stone
Elizabeth J. :   15 Jan 1855 - 22 Feb 1913, Mother

Hollon Brock :   5 Jul 1809 - 25 Mar 1904

Clarkey Rogers : [no other data]

Robert E. Eatmon :   1 Sep 1871 - 22 Jun 1938, Father

Esther B. Eatmon :   21 Mar 1893 - 31 Oct 1975, Mother

Raymond A. Eatmon :   7 Oct 1955 - 18 Oct 1955

Baby Boy Bell :   28 Feb 1957
   same stone
Mary Beth Bell :   9 Jan 1976, "Son & dau. of Donnell & Edna Bell"

Thomas Smith :   1856 - 1926, Father

Susan E. Adkinson, wife of Thomas Smith : 1860 - 1934, Mother

Katie Peare Blackmon :   7 Nov 1925 - 13 Jan 1926

Mabel Frances Blackmon :   28 May 1928 - 17 Jul 1928

MM unreadable

Burk H. Barnett :   1 Mar 1884 - 14 Aug 1936, Father
   same stone
Stella Wood :   3 Oct 1895 - 9 JUn 1950, Mother

31. PEARSELL CEMETERY (D-1)
      Located on SR 1004, .3 mile south of the junction with NC 403,
      on the east side of the road in a field.

Eugene Pearsell :   30 Jun 1880 - 15 Jun 1949

32. WHITFIELD CEMETERY (D-1)
      Located on SR 1004, 1.1 miles south of the intersection with NC 403,
      .5 mile off the east side on a farm road.

J.P. Whitfield :   17 Jun 1834 - 7 Jun 1921

Dan Whitfield :   Died 1953, [no age]

33. JONES CEMETERY (D-1)
     Located on SR 150Ī, on the south side of the road at the junction
     with SR 1528, in a field.

Rachel W., wife of M.B. Jones : [no dates]
   same stone
Ella Jones, dau. of M.B. & L.Jones : 27 Feb 1876 - 6 Apr 1884
   same stone
Elijah F. Jones and Mary F. Jones, son and dau. of
   R.W. & M.B. Jones : [no dates]

Tom Bennett, son of Tom & Nancy Bennett : 2 Jul 1899 - 25 Dec 1910

Barbara Loftin : 21 Sep 1864 - 25 Nov 1928, Mother

Robert W. Gough : 9 Feb 1839 - 5 Aug 1911

Thaddeus Jones : 20 Jul 1834 - 23 Mar 1904

Thaddeus Jones : 11 Dec 1919 - 21 Jun 1920

Festeus T. Jones, son of Thaddeus & Emma Jones
   13 Jan 1904 - 22 Apr 1913

[Several other graves without markers]

34. OUTLAW CEMETERY (G-2)
     Located on SR 1533, at the junction with NC 111, on the NE corner.

Paul Outlaw : 9 Sep 1889 - 3 Nov 1952
   same stone
Donnie : 15 Jun 1891 - n.d.

Mathew Lafayette Outlaw : 11 Jan 1861 - 29 May 1945
   same stone
Joseph Ida Outlaw : 12 Mar 1870 - 10 Jan 1951

Lena Bell Outlaw, dau. of A.G. & Katie Outlaw :
   7 Feb 1902 - 22 Jun 1905

Donald Erie Outlaw, son of A.G. & Katie Outlaw :
   31 Oct 1925 - 2 Jul 1930

Alonzo G. Outlaw : 28 Jan 1868 - 24 Jan 1937

Katie O. Outlaw : 17 Sep 1891 - 24 Oct 1972

35. OUTLAW CEMETERY (G-2)
     Located on SR 1533, .6 mile north of the junction with NC 111,
     .1 mile off the east side of the road.

Infant dau. of J.H. & Wineferd Outlaw : 1893

Alpha Mae Outlaw, dau. of J.H. & Wineferd Outlaw :
    12 Sep 1900 - 16 Apr 1915

Alfred James Outlaw, son of J.H. & Wineferd Outlaw :
    27 May 1898 - 10 Nov 1918

John Henry Outlaw : 9 May 1871 - 6 Feb 1940
    same stone
Wineferd Potter : 2 Sep 1873 - 24 Mar 1952

Henry S. Robinson : 3 Feb 1924 - 12 May 1952,
    NC PFC 34 ENGR COMBAT BN WWII

Ivey B. Sutton : 20 Mar 1888 - 16 Jan 1942, Father
    same stone
Patience E. : 14 Jul 1890 - 15 Sep 1950, Mother

Thomas A. Sutton, infant son of Ivey & Patience Sutton : 15 Mar 1928

L.W. Outlaw : 23 Oct 1876 - 11 Nov 1948

D.J. Outlaw : 11 Jan 1882 - 24 Aug 1904

Noah Outlaw : 7 Nov 1867 - May 1892

Lannie D. Outlaw : 9 Jun 1874 - 25 Jul 1942

O.E. Outlaw : 24 Dec 1842 - 7 Mar 1891, Mother

John E. Outlaw, CO A 45 NC INF CSA

Lena Sutton, dau. of J.H. & Lena Sutton : [no dates]

Infant dau. of T.H. & Patience Sutton

Infant son of T.H. & Patience Sutton

Claudie H. Outlaw : 17 Oct 1877 - 1878

Francis Outlaw : 2 Dec 1879 - 1880

George L. Outlaw : 14 Aug 1885 - 1886

George W. Outlaw : 3 Feb 1850 - 5 Feb 1928, Father
    same stone
Charlotte : 4 May 1850 - 19 May 1932, Mother

Infant of Clara F. & Luther Outlaw : 18 Feb 1932

Infant dau. of Moses T. & Edith Mewborn : 29 Oct 1920

Infant son of Moses T. & Edith Mewborn : 13 Jul 1910

Mary E. Outlaw, wife of Fred Outlaw : 10 May 1845 - 28 Jul 1878

[Three blank stones]

Thomas H. Sutton : 11 Dec 1858 – 9 Jun 1936, Father

Patience, wife of T.H. Sutton : 24 Jun 1855 – 3 May 1925, Mother

Daniel Kirby Sutton, son of Thomas H. & Patience Sutton :
    2 Oct 1895 – 13 Sep 1907

Major W. Sutton : 24 Aug 1884 – 30 Nov 1969, Father

Lillian Adell, wife of M.W. Sutton : 9 Apr 1888 – 8 Apr 1927, Mother

Randolph J. Outlaw, son of H.A. & Bettie H. Outlaw :
    8 Mar 1897 – 27 Dec 1936

Bettie Harper Outlaw : 7 Oct 1871 – 30 Jul 1958

Henry A. Outlaw : 10 Feb 1882 – 13 May 1921

Elizabeth J., wife of Lewis Outlaw : 21 May 1824 – 15 Jul 1891

Lewis Outlaw : 30 Sep 1809 – 8 Apr 1886

36. WHITFIELD CEMETERY (G-2)
        Located on NC 111, .2 mile south of the junction with SR 1533,
        .2 mile off the road on the south side.

Jasper Whitfield, son of W.J. & Likie Whitfield :
    23 Dec 1877 – 7 Aug 1899

Likie Whitfield, wife of W.J. Whitfield : 27 Jun 1853 – 3 Jun 1909

W.J. Whitfield : 18 Nov 1851 – 12 Jan 1912

Adline, wife of W.J. Whitfield : 27 May 1845 – 11 Jul 1921

Alton (Abbie) Outlaw : 1 Dec 1912 – 2 Jan 1959

Isaac Vance Outlaw : 24 Sep 1876 – 13 Nov 1955
    same stone
Ina Whitfield : 29 Nov 1879 – 12 May 1953

Maud Outlaw, dau. of I.V. & Ina Outlaw : 2 Jan 1902 – 9 Nov 1919

Ralph W. Outlaw : 13 Oct 1902 – 27 Jun 1951

Milton Outlaw : 17 May 1910 – 5 Jul 1966

37. NUNN CEMETERY (G-1)
      Located on SR 1535, .3 mile west of the intersection with
      SR 1534, on the south side of the road at the county line.

   Henry C. Nunn, son of W.F. & Mary E. Nunn :
      26 Jul 1856 - 5 Oct 1856

   John W. Nunn, son of Wm. F. & Mary E. Nunn :
      4 Jul 1853 - 23 Aug 1854

   Mary Elizabeth Nunn, wife of William F. Nunn :
      2 Sep 1829 - [stone broken]

38. CAPT. JAMES OUTLAW MEMORIAL MARKER   (G-2)
      Located at Outlaws Bridge Crossroad, (intersection of NC 111 & SR 1306)

                       Capt. James Outlaw
                          1744-1826

                   Elizabeth Grady, his wife

         "Original settlers lived and buried near this spot"

                          Children

                 Edward   Mary
                 John   Patience
                 James, Jr.   Elizabeth
                 Alexander   Charity
                 William   Nancy
                       Lewis

39. OUTLAW CEMETERY (G-2)
      Located on SR 1562, .2 mile north of the junction with NC 111,
      on the west side of the road.

   James Romie Outlaw : 5 Nov 1926 - 29 Oct 1973, US NAVY

   Georgia G., wife of James B. Outlaw : 26 Jul 1903 - 4 Feb 1975

   James Bryant Outlaw : 10 Oct 1902 - 17 Nov 1976

   Bryant T. Outlaw : 8 Jul 1856 - 12 Mar 1911

   Lossie I, wife of B.T. Outlaw : 1 Mar 1866 - 19 Jul 1920

   Three infant sons of J.C. & Ella S. Grady : [no dates]

Needham Bryan Outlaw : 6 Nov 1844 - 1 Mar 1930
    same stone "And Wives"
Penelope Outlaw : 8 Mar 1843 - 19 Jul 1882
    same stone
Annie Collier Whitfield : 21 Aug 1862 - 17 Aug 1900

Needham B. Outlaw, CO I 66 NC INF CSA

Jeff & Jack Outlaw, infant sons of Needham Bryan & Annie Whitfield Outlaw :
    [no dates]

Smithy & Daisy Outlaw, infant daus. of Needham Bryan & Penelope O. Outlaw :
    [no dates]

Betty Cobb Outlaw : 17 Jul 1897 - 15 Nov 1927

Nathalie Elizabeth Outlaw, dau. of N.B. & Annie W. Outlaw :
    11 Mar 1884 - 29 Jun 1973, Sister

Richard H. Outlaw : 8 Jun 1892 - 31 Jul 1976,
    Husband of Grace Smith Outlaw

Grace Smith Outlaw : 12 Jul 1887 - 10 Feb 1967,
    Wife of Richard Harding Outlaw

Johnnie Allen Quinn : 15 Apr 1890 - 14 Jun 1939, Father
    same stone
Bessie O. Q. Merritt : 15 May 1899 - 14 Dec 1974, Mother

MM unreadable

William D. Dupree : 30 Oct 1911 - 17 Feb 1974, NC PFC US ARMY WWII

40. STROUD CEMETERY (H-2)
    Located on N.C. 903,.2 mile north of the Albertson community,
    on the west side of the road.

Patsy Jewel Stroud, dau. of Needham & Edna Stroud :
    30 Aug 1942 - 3 Jan 1943

Lester Lee Britt, Sr. : 31 Oct 1910 - 18 Oct 1974
    same stone
Margaret Stroud : 21 Sep 1915 - n.d.

Frederick Grady : 22 Feb 1863 - 31 Oct 1931
    same stone
Edith S. : 20 Apr 1877 - 8 Jul 1975

Lester Lee Britt, Jr. : 9 Oct 1934 - 8 May 1961
    same stone
Jean Garner : 15 Jun 1938 - n.d.

Owen Stroud :   24 Mar 1882 – 29 Aug 1940

Infant son of Lester & Margaret Britt : [no dates]

Doris M. Stroud, dau. of Owen & Mannie Stroud : [no dates]

Elizabeth S. Hussey :   15 Mar 1875 – 24 Mar 1947

Kator B. Hussey :   1873 – 1923

Jeremiah Stroud, son of I.T. & Esther P. Stroud :
     12 Oct 1924 – 8 Aug 1940

Rev. Isaac Thomas Stroud :   22 May 1890 – 22 Jun 1981
     same stone
Esther Pease :   3 Aug 1894 – 21 Oct 1978

Hugh Stroud :   8 Feb 1886 – 18 Nov 1961, Father
     same stone
Mannie P. :   13 Oct 1893 – 6 Nov 1964, Mother

Clyde Stroud :   13 Jul 1922 – 7 Dec 1957, NC PFC US ARMY WWII

Ida W. Stroud : 10 Dec 1895 – 16 Jan 1972

Egbert Stroud :   16 Sep 1879 – 19 Nov 1943, Father

Fannie M., wife of Isaac Stroud : 11 Aug 1853 – 21 Jan 1945

Isaac Stroud :   12 Mar 1853 – 27 Jul 1928

Benjamin F. Stroud, son of Isaac & Fannie Stroud :
     6 Nov 1894 – 10 Mar 1905

Albert Stroud, son of Isaac & Fannie Stroud :
     26 May 1892 – 11 Sep 1904

Infant son of Barney & Marie Stroud ;   9 Jul 1921

Marie Young, wife of Barney Stroud : 17 Apr 1894 – 27 Jan 1921

Barney Stroud : 9 Nov 1891 – 22 May 1944, NC SGT QM CORPS

Carrie G., wife of Barney Stroud :   12 May 1892 – 7 May 1971, Mother

Glenn M. Stroud : 23 Sep 1922 – 11 Jul 1972, NC CPL US ARMY WWII

Lyda S., wife of Thurman Stroud : 12 Apr 1922 – 17 Jun 1972

William I. Sutton : 23 Feb 1872 – 10 Aug 1944, Father
     same stone
Kittie S. :   24 Oct 1883 – 26 Jan 1977, Mother

Fonnie Sutton, dau. of W.I. & Kittie Sutton : 1 Aug 1906 – 30 Sep 1909

Henry Sutton, son of W.I. & Kittie Sutton : 11 Jun 1919

E. Elane Ketcham : 2 Jan 1928 - 8 Dec 1931

Ethel K. Bequis : 29 May 1904 - 22 Sep 1943, Mother

John E. Stroud : 9 Jan 1872 - 24 Jan 1948
    same stone
Mary M. : 22 Feb 1881 - 22 Jan 1957

41. SIMMONS CEMETERY (G-2)
    Located on SR 1532, .4 mile south of the junction with NC 111,
    on the east side of the road.

Theodore R. Simmons, son of N.D. & Addie L. Simmons :
    26 Aug 1898 - 17 Jan 1919

Nathan D. Simmons : 5 Oct 1858 - 26 Jul 1922
    same stone
Addie L. : 3 Apr 1868 - 21 Jan 1923

W.H. (Tom) Kelly : 10 Jul 1881 - 26 Dec 1933
    same stone
Bertie O. Simmons : 14 Nov 1894 - 4 Aug 1981

Lillie C. Nunn : 1869 - 1934

42. HALSO-BATTS CEMETERY (R-4)
    Located on NC 50, 2.4 miles south of Chinquapin at the second
    junction with the loop road SR 1971, on the west side of the road.

Lois B., wife of Rudy Batts : 5 Dec 1949 - 18 Oct 1971

Robert L. Brown : 4 Nov 1923 - 19 Oct 1951, NC PFC 18 BN IRTC WWII

Ethel W., wife of S.A. Brown : 22 Feb 1889 - 3 Dec 1970

S.A. Brown : 7 Apr 1880 - 29 Oct 1947

Martha C., wife of W.H. Batts : 24 Mar 1855 - 31 Dec 1938

Clender Batchelor : 10 Apr 1893 - 19 Oct 1948
    same stone
Lillie Belle : 15 Mar 1897 - 21 Feb 1980

Beulah Batts : 5 Oct 1892 - 15 Apr 1976

Rachel L., wife of W.F. Batts : 22 Oct 1906 - 12 Dec 1949

Mary Elizabeth Batts, dau. of W.F. & Rachel Batts :
    16 Feb 1932 - 16 Sep 1936

Mary Elizabeth Batts :   28 Aug 1858 – 23 Aug 1924

Burl S. Batts :   26 Oct 1852 – 20 Oct 1934

Dora E., wife of Jesse Batts : 18 Mar 1897 – 6 Aug 1926

Jesse Batts :   13 Dec 1894 – 26 Jun 1939

John Ivey Batts : 15 Jun 1888 – 26 May 1963, Father
    same stone
Lula :   29 Jan 1891 – 26 Dec 1961, Mother

Joy Wood :   20 Apr 1882 – 23 Jun 1954
    same stone
Mary B. :   11 Mar 1893 – 12 May 1964

George N. Futrell :   27 Jan 1894 – 12 Nov 1949, Daddy

Bettie Batts, wife of George N. Futrell : 29 Dec 1896 – 13 Sep 1948, Mama

John D. Batts : 29 Mar 1850 – 24 Oct 1935

Beulah Pickett :   11 Mar 1893 – 20 NOv 1921

Sarah Magaline Wood :   20 May 1926 – 20 May 1926

Eldridge Jones :   5 Feb 1877 – 22 Nov 1944
    same stone
Minnie Whaley, his wife :   19 Dec 1882 – n.d.

Betty Alberta Whaley :   31 Dec 1915 – 23 Mar 1982

Hazel Glenn Whaley : 27 Jun 1918 – 25 Oct 1977, PFC US ARMY WWII

Ida Halso Whaley :   22 Feb 1881 – 4 Nov 1969
    same stone
Empie J. Whaley :   21 Nov 1886 – 8 Dec 1958

Precilla Williams :   11 Nov 1877 – 16 Dec 1940

Baby Williams :   b.&d. 9 Nov 1953

Martha E. Whaley, wife of J.R. Whaley : 15 Oct 1849 – 22 May 1921

James R. Whaley :   16 Oct 1861 – 4 Jul 1937

James Franklin Whaley :   20 May 1914 – 26 Sep 1961

Loy Leonadas Martin : 30 Sep 1895 – 12 May 1982, US ARMY WWII

Dave William Raynor : 12 Sep 1919 – 25 Jan 1969, NC SSGT US MARINE CORPS WWII

James H. Halso, son of J.G. & E.A. Halso : 29 Oct 1873 – 15 Dec 1897

Elizabeth A. Batts, wife of Robert James : 26 Oct 1847 – 27 Nov 1936

Robert James : 12 Apr 1847 – 1 Jan 1915

MM unreadable

Lonie B. James : 1890 – 1983, MM

Henrietta Lanier : 12 Sep 1880 – 27 Jan 1917 , Sister

Kattie Alma Halso, dau. of Mr. & Mrs. J.W. Halso : 1900 – 1901

Eliza Elizabeth Halso, dau. of Mr. & Mrs. J.W. Halso : 1897 – 1898

John W. Halso : 3 Jan 1872 – 12 Sep 1914, Father

Palmetto Halso, wife of John Halso : 24 Spe 1880 – 26 Mar 1961

Lou Ella Halso : 13 Dec 1910 – 16 Dec 1935, Daughter

Reynold Halso : 20 Apr 1902 – 25 Jul 1962, Father
       same stone
Estella R. : 3 May 1912 – n.d., Mother

Elizabeth Parker, wife of Jeremiah Lanier :
       12 Dec 1847 – 28 Feb 1925

Jeremiah Lanier : 1 May 1851 – 9 Sep 1901, Father

Norman Halso, son of Mr. & Mrs J.D. Halso : b. & d. 25 Nov 1944

Marie Halso, dau. of Mr. & Mrs. J.D. Halso : b. &d. 28 Sep 1942

John Dewey Halso : 1907 – 1950
       same stone
Ada Charlotte : 1912 – 1954

43. JAMES CEMETERY   (S-5)
       Located at the Cypress Creek Crossroad, .2 mile west of the
       intersection of SR 1828 & SR 1827, in a field.

R.F. Cavenaugh : 20 Nov 1935 – 2 Feb 1936

Infant son of R.M. & M.E. Cavenaugh : [no dates]

R.M. Cavenaugh : 17 Feb 1833 – 29 Dec 1927

O.D. Cavenaugh : 5 Jul 1895 – 29 Jun 1920

L.D. Brown : 6 Aug 1850 – 15 Jun 1918

Annie C., wife of S.D. Brown : 23 Oct 1848 – 20 Dec 1934

Infant son of S.D. & Annie C. Brown : [no dates]

David James : 13 Feb 1838 - 28 Feb 1865

Barbara James, wife of Isaac James : Died Mar 1860, Age 60 years

Isaac James : 1801 - 24 Nov 1854
    [Several other graves with unreadable wooden markers]

44. RAYNOR CEMETERY (T-5)
    Located on SR 1826, .9 mile north of the Cypress Creek Crossroad,
    .1 mile off the road on the west side, at edge of woods.

Mary Raynor, wife of Lewis C. Raynor : 30 Jun 1860 - 10 Feb 1902

Lewis C. Raynor : 31 Jul 1858 - 1 Feb 1934

Rachel F. Raynor, wife of L.C. Raynor : 29 Jul 1868 - 10 Apr 1962
    [Several other graves here with unreadable wooden markers]

45. TORRANS CEMETERY (M-1)
    Located on SR 1107, 1 mile north of the intersection with SR 1114,
    .3 mile off the road on the east side in a field.

Thomas K. Torrans, CO A 36 NC STATE TROOPS CSA

Samuel C. Torrans, CO K 9 NC STATE TROOPS CSA
    [Several other graves without markers]

46. HOLLINGSWORTH CEMETERY (M-1)
    Located on SR 1909, .5 mile east of the junction with US 117,
    .4 mile south of the road in the edge of the woods.

K.E. Hollingsworth : 3 Jun 1860 - 21 Jan 1928
    same stone
Ezra Alice Johnson, wife of K.E. Hollingsworth : 18 Dec 1866 - 22 Oct 1938

Virginia Lenora Hollingsworth, dau. of K.E. & E.A. Hollingsworth :
    1 Nov 1901 - 20 Feb 1907

Infant son of K.E. & E.A. Hollingsworth : 10 May 1912 - 5 Oct 1912

Kilby Hollingsworth : 15 Mar 1905, Age 83-2

Mary Eliser, wife of Kilby Hollingsworth : 11 Jan 1826 - 16 Nov 1907

Infant son of E.D. & Sallie Hollingsworth : 31 Mar 1920

Hettie F. Bass, dau. of W.H. & Mary J. Bass : 14 Sep 1870 - 28 Mar 1920

Julia Jones Bass, son of W.H. & Mary J. Bass : 20 Sep 1888 - 8 Dec 1902

Mary Julia Bass, wife of William H. Bass : 6 Jan 1842 - 14 Feb 1908

William H. Bass : 8 Dec 1838 - 7 Dec 1925, SGT CO A 43 NC INF CSA

Richard Gordon, son of M. & Susie Gordon : 15 May 1893 - 8 Jan 1904

Mary A. Hollingsworth, dau. of A. & S.J. Hollingsworth :
    17 Feb 1853 - 1 Apr 1853, Brother & Sister

Alfred Hollingsworth, husband of S.J. Hollingsworth :
    1 May 1820 - 14 Jan 1891

Sarah Jane, wife of Alfred Hollingsworth : 2 Dec 1835 - 3 Mar 1905

Susan A. Hollingsworth , dau. of Alfred & S.J. Hollingsworth :
    22 Jun 1866 - 19 Feb 1906

John Owen Hollingsworth, son of Alfred & S.J. Hollingsworth :
    20 Apr 1871 - 31 May 1901

Daughter of Fred O. & Pearl Hollingsworth : 8 Dec 1922 - 16 Jun 1924

47. THOMAS CEMETERY (N-2)
    Located on SR 1911,.3 mile south of the junction with SR 1003,
    .1 mile east of road in a field.

Charlie Thomas : 18 Oct 1870 - 29 Dec 1924

Margaret C. Thomas : 10 May 1882 - 21 Oct 1938

48. RACKLEY CEMETERY   (O-2)
    Located on SR 1912, .8 mile west from the junction with NC 11,
    on the north side of the road.

Dora V. Robinson, wife of F.P. Rackley : 19 Mar 1860 - 2 Jul 1900

Franklin P. Rackley : 6 Feb 1853 - 20 Mar 1920, Father

Zilpha J. Rackley, wife of John C. Rackley : 28 Nov 1829 - 16 Jul 1880

J.A. Rackley, son of J.C. & Z.J. Rackley : 11 Oct 1857 - 26 Jun 1894

49. BLANTON CEMETERY (N-6)
     Located on SR 1154, 1.1 miles south of the junction with NC 41,
     .1 mile east of the road in a field.

W.A. Heath : 22 Jul 1845 - 17 May 1910

Susan E. Blanton, wife of W.A. Heath : 12 May 1845 - 21 Apr 1909

Phebty Carolin Blanton : 22 Feb 1849 - 12 Jan 1876

J.H.B. [on Footstone]

[Broken homemade marker, unreadable, made like the one next to it, was next.

Mary Blanton : 24 Jul 1820 - 22 Mar 1880
     [Several other unmarked graves here]

50. BLACKMORE CEMETERY (A-4)
     Located on SR 1342, .2 mile east from the junction with SR 1340,
     on the south side of the road.

Howard Edward Blackmore : 2 Sep 1878 - 18 Jan 1965

Harold Kenneth Brown, son of Ira Estella B. Brown:
     6 Jul 1915 - 20 Nov 1917

Mary J., wife of Harold E. Blackmore : 6 Jun 1846 - 6 Feb 1924

Harold E. Blackmore : 24 Nov 1840 - 9 Apr 1905

Buckner L. Blackmore : 4 Jul 1844 - 23 Sep 1921

Julia Sarepta, wife of Buckner L. Blackmore : 1 Jun 1847 - 1 Dec 1918

Emmett B. Blackmore : 13 Mar 1887 - 26 Sep 1910

Mary Aliff Blackmore : 27 May 1875 - 17 Jun 1877

Julia S. Blackmore : 28 Nov 1877 - 28 Nov 1877

Romulus W. Blackmore : 26 Jun 1872 - 19 May 1963

Harold Blackmore : 12 May 1801 - 22 Apr 1885

William A. Whitley : 2 Jan 1861 - 14 Oct 1912

Janey Sansbury Blackmore : 21 Feb 1887 - 3 Mar 1967

Willie R. Blackmore : 21 Mar 1877 - 13 Jan 1955
     "A Justice of the Peace for 30 years"

I.F. Blackmore : 24 Mar 1852 - 31 Jan 1929

Mary A., wife of I.F.Blackmore : 30 Jul 1844 - 15 Jun 1898

Wentworth F. Blackmore : 6 Oct 1875 - 28 May 1939

Infant son of Willie & Janie S. Blackmore : Apr 1912

Infant son of Willie & Janie S. Blackmore : Oct 1914

Janie Belle Blackmore : 18 Apr 1922 - 21 Jan 1961
    "Singer, Poet, Sufferer Triumphant"

Richard E. Blackmore : 31 Oct 1854 - 11 Dec 1899

Annie Mariah Hatcher : 1818 - 25 Feb 1907

Fedorah O.O. Blackmore : 25 Sep 1847 - 8 Aug 1917

51. GRADY CEMETERY (H-3)
        Located on SR 1546, 1.5 miles east from the junction with NC 111,
        on the north side of the road.

Eliza Catherine Grady : 27 Mar 1867 - 5 Dec 1952

Robert J. Grady, son of J. McR. & Mary Grady :
    13 May 1898 - 20 Aug 1899

John Grady : 1 Oct 1818 - 19 Oct 1898

Celie Grady, dau. of Joshua Ezzell, wife of John Grady :
    23 Aug 1830 - 28 Sep 1884

William J. Grady : 22 Jun 1865 - 11 Aug 1949

Katie V. Grady, dau. of B.D. & S.E. Ford, wife of W.J. Grady :
    28 Nov 1868 - 29 Apr 1964

Ethel M. Grady, dau. of J.McR. & Mary Grady : 12 May 1892 - 31 May 1893

Byron M. Grady, son of W.J. & K.V. Grady : 5 Sep 1900 - 17 Aug 1913

52. SUTTON CEMETERY (B-2)
        Located on SR 1320, .8 mile NW of the junction with NC 403,
        .2 mile south of the road in a field.

Anna Kathrine Sutton, dau. of M.H. & Helen Sutton : 14 Sep 1925 - 1 Dec 1928

Pamlia Ann Miller : 1970 - 1970

Leonard L. Jinnette :   21 Jul 1893 - 25 Nov 1951

Henry Carl Jinnette :   1891 - 1941

Mary Etta Brogden :   26 Jan 1869 - 3 Oct 1949

William H. Jennette :   23 Sep 1858 - 16 Dec 1896

Floyd L. Jennette :   21 Oct 1889 - 9 Jul 1890

Edna L. Jennette :   27 Mar 1895 - 1 Dec 1918

Thaddeus Whitney Barbrey, son of Allen & Betsey Barbrey :
    1 Aug 1865 - 12 Dec 1907

Hettie M. Sutton Barbrey Powell : 12 Dec 1873 - 14 Aug 1964

Cecil Allen Barbrey, son of Thad. & Hettie Barbrey :
    2 Jan 1899 - 25 Oct 1909

Sarah Elva Barbrey, dau. of Thad. & Hettie Barbrey :
    27 Sep 1900 - 10 Jan 1901

Laurence S. Brogden, son of D.B. & M.E. Brogden :
    12 Sep 1907 - 1 Dec 1935

Carrie J. Sutton, wife of M.O. Summerlin : 30 Mar 1881 - 3 Jun 1913
    Married 27 Mar 1910

Cora Sutton, dau. of O.W. & E.J. Sutton : 11 Apr 1883 - 13 Jan 1904

Emma L. Sutton, dau. of O.W. & E.J. Sutton : 11 Oct 1866 - 21 Feb 1882

William Oswin Sutton, son of Geo. T. & Lucy L.Sutton :
    16 Sep 1900 - 16 Apr 1906

O.W. Sutton, Jr., son of E.B. & F.L. Sutton : 2 Sep 1907 - 16 Sep 1908

Sara Carrie Sutton, dau. of E.B. & F.L. Sutton : 22 Aug 1909 - 3 Dec 1910

Infant son of E.B. & F.L. Sutton : 3 Nov 1911 - 6 Nov 1911

Frances Olivia Sutton, dau. of E.B. & F.L. Sutton : 23 Oct 1912 - 18 Nov 19

Edward B. Sutton :   24 Jul 1877 - 4 Nov 1933
    same stone
Fannie Hood :   15 Apr 1881 - 27 Dec 1965

O.W. Sutton :   2 Aug 1834 - 7 Nov 1917, Father
    same stone
Elva Jane :   17 Dec 1843 - 22 Oct 1901, Mother

Oswin W. Sutton, SGT CO F 1 NC ARTY CSA

Joel Loftin : 13 May 1818 - 2 Feb 1879 [Masonic Emblem]

Mary, wife of William H. Jones : 21 Aug 1816 - 12 May 1853

Elisha Herring : 1 May 1775 - 12 Oct 1858

*Elisha Herring, son of Elisha & Mary Herring : 27 Jan 1827 - 16 Aug 1859

* From the records of Mrs. H.B. Kornegay, Sr., recorded in 1968. This
  marker was not present in 1983.

53. BRICE CEMETERY (Supplement)* (O-5)
        Located on NC 41, 1.3 miles east of the intersection with NC 11,
        (Tin City), on the south side of the road.

    *NOTE : These records are a supplement to the Brice Cemetery previously
             recorded by Leora H. McEachern in DUPLIN COUNTY GRAVESTONE RECORDS,
             Vol. 8, page 29, 1978. They are from the files of Mr. Cecil
             Bradshaw.

G.F. Dempsey : 23 Jan 1830 - 25 Dec 1909

Ann L. Dempsey : 4 Jul 1841 - 31 Jul 1881

Francis Brice : 16 Mar 1816 - 9 Jun 1881

Margaret Brice : 5 Mar 1819 - 8 Mar 1879

Sarah W. Brice : 12 Nov 1846 - 8 Jun 1862

William Dewey Brice : 29 Mar 1916 - 26 Oct 1955
        NC PFC BTRY C 311 FIELD ARTY BN WWII

Margaret E. Brice, wife of L.J. Batts : 1 Oct 1870 - 14 Jun 1921

John J. Brice : 26 Dec 1844 - 16 Jan 1899
        same stone
Mary Susan Bryant, his wife : 23 Oct 1841 - 2 Jun 1918

George Vance Brice : 12 Sep 1878 - 12 Jun 1929
        same stone
Nancy Watson : 26 Mar 1892 - 10 Aug 1982

Daniel A. Norris : 6 Jun 1901 - 29 Jan 1970
        same stone
Ethelyn B. : 6 Aug 1913 - n.d.

Joseph L. Carter : 15 Mar 1892 - 13 Jun 1961

Daisy C. Carter : 14 Jul 1882 - 21 Feb 1940

Oscar S. Carter : 28 Mar 1897 - 4 Nov 1929
        same stone
Viola T. Carter : 21 Nov 1899 - n.d.

Rev. T.H. Carter : 26 Sep 1843 – 7 Apr 1915

Sarah E. Carter : 26 Nov 1853 – 26 Dec 1927

Archie W. Carter : 15 Nov 1890 – 15 Oct 1957
    NC CPL 50 CO 5 GP MG TNG CEN WWI

Henry Carter, son of T.H. & Sarah E. Carter : 18 Mar 1871 – 14 Apr 1873

Molly Carter, dau. of T.H. & Sarah E. CArter :
    17 JUn 1873 – 22 Nov 1877

Winnie Dell Carter, dau. of of T.H. & Sarah E. Carter :
    15 Jan 1883 – 12 Dec 1885

Willie Carter, son of T.H. & Sarah E. Carter : 15 Jun 1885 – 13 Aug 1885

Willie T. Carter, son of T.H. & Emma H. Carter :
    9 Mar 1904 – 18 Aug 1940

Thomas H. Carter, Jr. : 8 Mar 1877 – 5 Oct 1949
    same stone
Emma H. : 5 Jan 1883 – 9 Mar 1960

Rayford H. Carter : 1916 – 1965
    same stone
Doris H. : 1930 – n.d.

James W. Moore : 3 Feb 1879 – 17 Nov 1938
    same stone
Betsey J. : 25 Feb 1883 – 12 Jun 1940

Cathrine E. Register, dau. of E.G. & Lela Register :
    18 Jul 1922 – 26 Oct 1922

O.W. Carter : 23 May 1849 – 26 Nov 1905
    same stone
Mary E. : 18 Apr 1858 – 6 Jan 1923

Mary Florence Brice, dau. of F.R. & O.W. Brice : 11 Feb 1913 – 13 May 1913

Stephen H. Murray : 31 Jan 1862 – 18 Dec 1927

Sarah M. Murray, wife of S.H. Murray : 25 Aug 1868 – 18 Nov 1911

P.S. Murray : 19 Nov 1898 – 2 May 1919

John I. Murray : 24 Nov 1892 – 13 Sep 1951
    same stone
Minnie D. : 8 Oct 1911 – n.d.

Infant dau. of Leona M. & Billy Teachey : 2 Sep 1961

Infant son of Leona M. & Billy Teachey : 14 Jan 1964 – 16 Jan 1964

B.J. Lanier :   1898 – 1967
     same stone
Bonnie Dell :   1896 – 1941

54. WHITMAN CEMETERY (F-3)
     Located on SR 1502, .1 mile north of the intersection with SR 1500,
     (Scotts Store Crossroad), on the east side of the road.

Barney W. Whitman :   23 Dec 1892 – 13 Jun 1966
     same stone
Doney H. :   19 Oct 1911 – 22 Mar 1978

Wright Whitman :   27 Jan 1861 – 2 Sep 1940
     same stone
Nancy Susan :   15 May 1865 – 24 Jul 1943

William Edward Jackson, son of W.J. & Norah Jackson :
     21 Sep 1924 – 6 Jan 1928

W.J. Jackson :   24 Nov 1879 – 28 Jun 1945
     same stone
Nora W. Jackson :   20 Sep 1890 – 1 Nov 1982

Charlie Franklin Jackson :   27 Nov 1919 – 24 May 1969
     NC PVT 1928 QM TRUCK CO WWII
     same stone
Evangeline :   16 Mar 1933 – 1 Sep 1978

C. Henry Jackson :   14 Jan 1901 – 29 Jul 1941
     same stone
Gertrude M. :   10 Sep 1905 – 11 Jul 1943

55. WHITFIELD CEMETERY (F-2)
     Located on SR 1519, .1 mile south of the junction with SR 1501,
     on the west side of the road, in a field.

Estelle Jones, wife of T.W. Garris : 27 Feb 1897 – 24 Jun 1923

Randolph Hinson :   28 Jul 1910

Ashley E. Tew, wife of Major Jones :   4 Sep 1863 – 14 Feb 1927

Major Jones :   15 Dec 1868 – 1 Jun 1905

J.D. Sutton :   Died 23 Mar 1920, Age 80 years

Chellis E. Sutton :   18 Mar 1836 – 11 Sep 1911

Edieth Whitfield, wife of J.D. Summerlin : 1 May 1843 – 10 Feb 1921

B.H. Whitfield :   11 Jul 1824 – 24 May 1887

56. GARNER CEMETERY (F-2)
        Located on SR 1528, .6 mile north of the junction with SR 1501,
        .3 mile east of the road on a farm road.

Furnander Price, wife of Joseph J. Garner : 17 Nov 1881 - 17 Nov 1904

Joel J. Garner : 27 Oct 1861 - 15 Jul 1917

Arnie Whitfield, wife of Joseph J. Garner : 17 Jan 1871 - 27 May 1901

Arnie Bell Garner, dau. of J.J. & Arnie W. Garner :
        15 Oct 1894 - 11 Aug 1898

Alice Udorah Garner, dau. of J.J. & Arnie W. Garner :
        23 Dec 1896 - 17 Feb 1914

J.J. Garner, Jr. : 17 Mar 1901 - 23 Feb 1921

Lola Garner, wife of D.J. Turner : 27 Aug 1898 - 6 Feb 1925

57. PRICE CEMETERY (F-2)
        Located on SR 1528, .6 mile north of the junction with SR 1501,
        .6 mile east on a farm road; (.3 mile east of previously cemetery).

John T. Price, Sr. : 30 Jan 1858 - 27 Jun 1920
Lula, wife of J.T. Price : 4 Oct 1875 - 18 Feb 1939

58. HOLMES CEMETERY (F-2)
        Located on SR 1528, .6 mile north of the junction with SR 1501,
        .6 mile east of road on a farm road, then .3 mile north of the
        previous cemetery on a dirt path in the woods.

Joel Holmes : 2 Jun 1878 - 6 Oct 1952

Gerutrude B. Garner, wife of Joel Holmes : 3 Jul 1879 - 10 May 1951

59. BROCK CEMETERY (D-2)
        Located on SR 1503, .3 mile east of the junction with SR 1500,
        on the north side of the road.

Jesse H. Brock : 12 Jan 1847 - 13 Mar 1914

Lucinda, wife of J.H. Brock :
        18 Nov 1849 - 20 Aug 1909

60. CARTER CEMETERY (C-2)
    Located on SR 1368, .1 mile north of the junction with SR 1367,
    on the west side of the road.

Calvin Lowell Carter, son of A.H. & Beatrice Carter :
    3 Aug 1943 - 21 Nov 1945

Infant son of A.H. & Beatrice Carter :   30 Oct 1937

Atlas Harvey Carter :   12 Jun 1905 - 9 May 1970
    same stone
Beatrice Williamson :   15 Nov 1906 - 2 Jul 1962

Ashford Carter :   11 Mar 1833 - 24 Nov 1903

Louise Holmes, wife of Ashford Carter :   1837 - Feb 1909

Mrs. Octavia Carter :   17 Aug 1960, Age 77 years, MM

61. SWINSON CEMETERY (C-2)
    Located on SR 1368, .8 mile south of the junction with SR 1367,
    .1 mile off the west side of the road in edge of woods.

Nancy, wife of Jesse Swinson : Died 18 Feb 1837, Age 79 years

Jesse Swinson : Died 17 Apr 1834, Age 75 years

[According to Mr. Randal Brock, owner of the property, the following
are also buried here, without any visible markers: James Auston Swinson;
Jesse & Nancy Walker-husband & wife; a Williams infant; Mary King Mercer
and her son Joe Mercer; and two Jackson girls. It is said that part of
this cemetery was used as a slave cemetery.]

62. McARTHUR CEMETERY (C-2)
    Located on SR 1357, .4 mile west of the junction with SR 1306,
    on the south side of the road, .1 mile in a field.

Charlie McArthur :   19 Sep 1871 - 22 Dec 1935
    same stone
Ora M. :   3 Apr 1878 - n.d.

MM unreadable

Linwood E. McArthur :   17 Dec 1923 - 16 Dec 1958

63. PRIDGEN CEMETERY   (C-2)
    Located on SR 1364, .6 mile E. of the junction with sR 1306, (Beautancus),
    on the north side of the road.

John William Pridgen :   25 Jan 1905 - 8 Dec 1963

Robert Morris Pridgen, son of John & Ethel Pridgen :
13 Jul 1952 - 10 May 1954

Nettie R. Pridgen : 1 Jun 1865 - 5 Jun 1924

Julius R. Jones : 11 Sep 1881 - 12 Nov 1951

64. STANFORD MEMORIAL MARKER   (O-1)
Located on NC 11, 1.3 miles south of the junction with SR 1003,
.1 mile off the west side of the road in a field.

NOTE: This memorial marker is to be relocated in the Routledge
Cemetery, Kenansville, NC

Rev. Samuel Stanford

"Born in Orange County, N.C. A Soldier in

the Revolution; Pastor of Grove Church

and President of Grove Academy from

1795 to 1833. Died in Duplin County 1833."

"Erected by Scott Stanford, a Grandson"

65. HENRY FAISON MEMORIAL MARKER (A-2)
Located in Faison, NC, two blocks west on Main St.from the railroad,
on the south side of the street.

Henry Faison
1744-1788

and his wife

Diana Griffin
1756-1828

"Progenitors of the Faison
family of Faison"

66. HERRING CEMETERY (F-4)
Located on SR 1306, .6 mile south of the junction with SR 1502,
(Red Hill), on the east side of Herring Marsh, in the edge of the woods.

Rachel, wife of Daniel Herring : Died 7 Jan 1856, Ag'd 56-10-20
"Left a husband and four children to mourn their lost. She was a
member of the Baptist Church-a professor religion for 30 years -
and died in the full hope of happy immortality."

Mollie, wife of F.A. Jones : 1865 - 1891

[There were many other graves here without markers.]

67. BOYETTE CEMETERY (A-5)
        Located on SR 1111, .3 mile south of the junction with NC 24,
        .1 mile east of the road, in the edge of the woods.

William Boyette : 1 Feb 1819 - 13 Jun 1892

MM unreadable

[Several other graves here without markers]

68. WILLIAMS CEMETERY (L-4)
        Located on SR 1100, .6 mile NW of the intersection with SR 1102,
        200 yards SW of the road in the woods.

Jas. Boney Williams : 21 Jan 1844 - 3 Mar 1911

Carrie Herring, wife of J.B. Williams : 24 Jul 1846 - 27 Oct 1936

69. KORNEGAY CEMETERY (G-3)
        Located on SR 1518, .1 mile south of the junction with SR 1519,
        on the east side of the road.

Robert D. Kornegay : 9 May 1852 - 12 Apr 1929

Eliza Cornella Kornegay : 7 Aug 1857 - 12 Jun 1937

Swannie Belle Kornegay : 14 Jun 1896 - 11 Mar 1918

70. GRADY CEMETERY (H-4)
        Located on NC 111, .3 mile north of the junction with NC 11,
        on the west side of the road, .2 mile in a field.

Henry G. Grady : 2 Dec 1803 - 14 Mar 1870

71. HERRING CEMETERY (H-1)
        Located on N.C. 903,.5 mile north of the intersection with SR 1306,
        .4 mile off the road on the west side, in a field.

John William Herring : 14 Oct 1868 - 27 May 1939
        same stone
Cuzzie Jane : 20 Nov 1881 - 10 Aug 1942

John B. Bizzell : 17 Sep 1894 - 5 Jun 1933
        same stone
Bessie E. : 9 Sep 1897 - n.d.

Laura E. Bizzell, dau. of J.B. & Bessie E. Bizzell : 29 Oct 1915 - 27 Aug 1916

Stephen A. Herring :   16 Apr 1833 - 3 Jan 1913
     same stone
Patience Herring :   22 Aug 1835 - 29 Jul 1906

Two wooden markers, unreadable

MM unreadable

Infant child of A.E. & Emma Tyndall : 26 Mar 1901 - 17 May 1902

L.J. Davenport :   6 Sep 1861 - 15 Jan 1914

Maggie O., wife of L.J. Davenport :   20 Apr 1857 - 30 Jun 1933

Infant son of J.O. & S.O. Guy :   8 Oct 1916 - 29 Oct 1916

"Buddy" Warren R. Woodard, Jr., son of W.R. & L.B. Woodard :
    6 Feb 1930 - 3 Oct 1934

Infant dau. of W.R. & L.B. Woodard :   1926

72. JONES CEMETERY (H-2)
    Located on SR 1537, .5 mile south of the junction with SR 1306,
on the west side of the road.

Willard A. Jones :   25 Apr 1915 - 9 Oct 1952

Amos J. Jones :   7 Jun 1893 - 6 Feb 1947

73. PHILLIPS CEMETERY (H-2)
    Located at the southern end of SR 1560, in a field.

Windol R. Watkins, son of W.R. & E. Watkins : 24 Dec 1911 - 19 Apr 1913

Susan, wife of Wm. I Quinn :   23 Sep 1858 - 15 Jan 1875

Ebby Phillips :   20 Jul 1875 - 2 Aug 1940

Mary A., wife of M.J. Phillips : 20 Jul 1838 - 19 Apr 1914

M.J. Phillips :   25 Oct 1832 - 18 Jul 1903

Rostion Phillips, son of J.J. & Girtie Phillips : b.&d. 30 May 1902

Julia Quinn, wife of W.C. Rouse :   27 Sep 1893 - 25 Jun 1928

Reba Lue Rouse, dau. of W.C. & J.Q. Rouse : 21 Mar 1926 - 23 Mar 1926

Infant son of W.C. & Julia Rouse :   b.&d. 16 Nov 1921

Infant son of W.C. & J.Q. Rouse : 10 Mar 1925

MM unreadable

MM unreadable

Infant son of Jesse & Pearl Quinn : b. & d. 31 Aug 1911

Infant twin daus. of Jesse & Pearl Quinn : b.& d. 16 Sep 1912

Two wooden markers, unreadable

W.I. Quinn : 13 Jul 1856 – 30 Mar 1918

Lucy, wife of W.I. Quinn : 12 Jan 1860 – 1 Oct 1905

[There were several other wooden markers, unreadable]

74. ALPHIN CEMETERY (H-2)
     Located on SR 1560, .2 mile south of the junction with SR 1537,
     on the west side of the road.

Mr. W.H. Honeycutt : 1914 – 1971

David Alphin : 26 May 1930 – 1 Apr 1965, Brother

75. WHITFIELD CEMETERY (G-2)
     Located on SR 1306, 1 mile NE from the junction with NC 111,
     (Outlaws Bridge Crossroad), .4 mile NW on a farm road in the woods.

Rachel J., wife of S.W. Peele : 14 Apr 1866 – 29 Jan 1938

S.W. Peele : 15 Jan 1853 – 19 Nov 1923

Infant grave : [no data]

Fannie Adell, wife of Johnie Whitfield : 2 Oct 1894 – 1 Jun 1928

Lucy Outlaw, wife of Lemuel H. Whitfield : 1848 – 1880

L.H. Whitfield, CO H 2 NC INF CSA

Rachel E. Outlaw, "Betty" : 18 Apr 1877 – 17 Oct 1950

Needham F. Outlaw : 2 Jun 1860 – 24 Mar 1940

76. STROUD CEMETERY (I-2)
     Located on SR 1541, .5 mile south of the junction with SR 1544,
     on the west side of the road in a field.

Lannie C. Stroud : 7 Sep 1932 – 11 Jun 1971, A3C US ARMY

Gordon Stroud : 12 Mar 1890 – 23 Jul 1971
    same stone
Annie T. :   24 Feb 1903 – n.d.

Effie Lee Stroud, dau. of Gordon & Annie Stroud :
    29 Jun 1926 – 11 May 1928

Mary Stroud, dau. of Gordon & Annie Stroud :
    29 Nov 1928 – 5 Jun 1933

Leslie Stroud, Jr. : 28 Nov 1929 – 17 Apr 1980

Nelma F. Stroud : 17 Jun 1927 – 28 Mar 1976

Charlie Stroud, son of Leslie & Nellie Stroud : 1 Mar 1926 – 25 Feb 1927

Leslie Stroud : 10 Apr 1901 – 5 Feb 1976
    same stone
Nellie Lee Stroud : 2 Nov 1906 – n.d.

Baby Boy Stroud : 14 Sep 1963, MM

Bertie Cora, wife of Owen Stroud : 23 Dec 1898 – 19 Jan 1943

Owen Stroud : 23 Mar 1892 – 15 Sep 1946, NC Teamsters, 1 PROV DEV REGT WWI

Baby Girl Stroud : 17 May 1960, MM

  _?_ rl Stroud : Jan 1961, MM

Betty Jean Stroud : 22 May 1944 [no other date]

Jagold Stroud, Jr. : 7 Jan 1958 – 22 Oct 1970

Jagold Stroud : 23 Jul 1909 – 26 Jul 1966

Infant of Ashley & Donnie Stroud : b. & d. 14 Sep 1933

Moten Harold Stroud, son of Ashley & Mattie Stroud :
    3 Jul 1922 – 26 Jun 1924

Albert Stroud, son of Ashley & Mattie Stroud :
    9 Dec 1919 – 3 Mar 1926

Mattie, wife of Ashley Stroud : 21 Nov 1880 – 22 Mar 1926

Ashley Stroud : 12 Feb 1877 – 6 Dec 1950, Father

Nancy W. Stroud, dau. of Owen & Sallie R. Stroud :
    18 May 1847 – 13 Apr 1921

Elcie A. Stroud, dau. of Owen & Sallie R. Stroud :
    4 May 1861 – 3 Sep 1945

Lannie Stroud, son of Jobe & Charlotte Stroud :
    20 Aug 1883 - 11 Feb 1921

Moten Stroud : 1 May 1898 - 26 Apr 1922

Jobe Stroud : 15 Nov 1854 - 1 Oct 1933

Charlotte E., wife of Jobe Stroud : 18 Jan 1861 - 7 Feb 1937

Oscar Stroud : 22 Aug 1886 - 8 Feb 1948

O'Neal "Billy" Bradshaw : 19 May 1943 - 8 Jan 1947

Infant son & dau. of Henry & Annie B. Lee : 29 May 1952

C. Raymond Stroud : 20 Apr 1886 - 23 Aug 1957
    same stone
Annie S. : 21 Dec 1895 - n.d.

Hazel Estell Stroud, dau. of Raymond & Annie Stroud :
    17 May 1923 - 21 Jul 1924

Robert Earl Turner : 17 Jun 1933 - 12 Jun 1960

Dolly Jane Elizabeth, wife of Durwood Turner : 23 Mar 1900 - 21 Jul 1941,Mother

Hollan A. West : 21 Nov 1855 - 3 Nov 1930

Robert Robinson : 12 Dec 1926 - 6 Oct 1977, Daddy
    same stone
Juanita : 13 May 1915 - n.d., Mama

Ronald Lane Hill, son of Cleveland & Mary J. Hill :
    28 Jul 1936 - 11 Jan 1943

Martin Turner : 17 Sep 1875 - 27 Jan 1945
    same stone
Mollie : 30 Jun 1880 - 21 Jul 1964

77. MALPASS CEMETERY (I-3)
    Located on SR 1541, .9 mile north of the junction with SR 1555,
    on the east side of the road, .1 mile in a field.

Troy Smith : 1896 - 1954

Mary S., wife of Allen Smith : 1 Oct 1859 - 18 May 1924

Allen Smith : 18 Feb 1856 - 28 Feb 1913

Charlie A. Smith, son of Allen & Mary S. Smith : 1 Dec 1897 - 3 Oct 1907

Delia Catherine, wife of John R. Herring : 20 May 1855 - 20 Jul 1932

Eddie L. Carter : 27 Mar 1887 – 1 Jun 1951, NC PVT CO A 357 INF WWI

L.H. Carter : 26 Jan 1846 – 28 Oct 1919

Nancy, wife of L.H. Carter : 9 Mar 1840 – 1 Oct 1934

Charlie Jane, wife of I.D. Langston : 25 Aug 1882 – 6 Sep 1934

Randolph Langston : 1916 – 1975

J.H. Taylor : 8 Jun 1852 – 6 Jun 1914

Wm. Malpass : 13 Dec 1863 – 24 Jul 1913

Carrie Malpass : 1907 – 1913

Myrtie, wife of George Carter : 7 Nov 1881 – 14 Jul 1923

Raymond Carter, son of Geo. & Myrtie Carter :
    14 Jul 1924 – 16 Feb 1925

George Carter : 25 Aug 1870 – 11 Jun 1940

J.M. Malpass : 25 Nov 1868 – 22 Dec 1932

Birtie T. Malpass, wife of Joel M. Malpass : 19 Aug 1875 – 30 Mar 1953, Mothe

Thurman Malpass, son of Joel & Birtie Malpass : 30 Jul 1908 – 12 Feb 1925

Stella May Malpass, dau. of Joel & Birtie Malpass :
    17 Jun 1912 – 12 Jan 1914

Stella Malpass, dau. of Joel & Birtie Malpass :
    4 May 1895 – 22 Sep 1907

Two MM, unreadable

Thurman Herring, son of Charlie & Della Herring : 9 Apr 1925 – 16 Jan 1931

Chancy Smith : 3 May 1853 – 5 Oct 1917

Polly Smith : 18 Jul 1865 – 8 Feb 1953

MM unreadable

Charlie Holland, husband of Wennieford Holland : 22 Dec 1856 – 7 Mar 1923

Winnie, wife of Charlie Holland : 29 Mar 1861 – 3 Jul 1933

78. GUY CEMETERY (I-3)
    Located on SR 1543, .3 mile north of the junction with SR 1546,
    .1 mile east of the road in a field.

Marion Nixon Guy, dau. of J.O. & S.O. Guy :
    15 Jul 1933 – 18 Jun 1934

John Owen Guy : 10 Jan 1881 – 24 Nov 1945
    same stone
Sadie Oda : 11 Mar 1891 – 8 Dec 1969

Ruth Jean Davis, infant dau. of W.H. & Ruth G. Davis : 17 Sep 1943

MM unreadable

79. SOUTHERLAND CEMETERY (C-3)
    Located on SR 1305, .4 mile south of the junction with SR 1306,
    on the east side of the road, .1 mile in edge of woods.

Stella E. Southerland, dau. of J.N. & E.T. Southerland :
    25 Feb 1877 – 13 Aug 1893

80. TAYLOR CEMETERY (A-1)
    Located on SR 1321, .6 mile west of the junction with SR 1302,
    on the north side of the road, .1 mile in a field.

Johnny C. Taylor : 13 Aug 1894 – 14 Nov 1894

81. WRIGHT CEMETERY (A-1)
    Located on SR 1321, .1 mile east of the Sampson County line,
    on the north side of the road.

Thomas Wright : Died 27 Oct 1846, Aged 84-10-24
[Daughters of the American Revolution, Richard Clinton Chapter, marker at grave]

Eliza, wife of Thomas Wright : Died 3 Mar 1849, Aged 71 years

Mary Ann Washington, wife of Richard Washington : 1 Aug 1802 – 29 Apr 1839

Thomas Wright : 10 Aug 1806 – 4 Jul 1887

Thomas B. Wright : 6 Oct 1834 – 25 Jul 1869

John D. Wright : 14 Dec 1842 – 20 Aug 1862
[Several other graves here, but no other markers found]

82. TAYLOR CEMETERY (A-1)
    Located on SR 1302, .1 mile NW from the junction with SR 1308,
    on the SW side of the road.

Susan W., wife of Croom [Strowd] : 23 Oct 1846 – 30 Aug 1914, Mother

Joseph Holland : 8 Sep 1808 – 26 Jan 1895

Nancy Jane Holland : 11 Sep 1828 - 8 Jan 1896

Elizabeth Taylor : 1 Aug 1838 - 8 Jan 1913

Isham U. Taylor : 1 Jul 1824 - 1 May 1894

Jesse K. Taylor :   30 Apr 1879 - 1 Aug 1885

83.BENNETT CEMETERY (A-1)
        Located on SR 1302, .1 mile NW of the junction with SR 1308,
        on the NE side of the road, in a field.

Granger G. Browning : 28 Jun 1903 - 13 Oct 1941

Robert James Browning : 13 Feb 1878 - 7 Oct 1952, Father
        same stone
Connie Eva Bennett : 6 Jun 1878 - n.d.

Wellie W. [Browing] : 1 Nov 1970 - 16 Oct 1972

Flossie B. Gordon : 26 Mar 1913 - 27 Dec 1966

Mary Barfield, wife of S.L. Bennett : 1833 - 1911

Infant dau. of R.J. & Connie Browning : b.&d. 14 Apr 1912

Georgie Grace Bennett, dau. of M.R. & V.E. Bennett :
        30 May 1901 - 24 Oct 1905

Octavia Bennett, wife of J.F. Sasser : 1871 - 1911

Mary Estelle Sasser, dau. of J.F. & O.I. Bennett : 6 Jul 1900 - 10 Jun 1901

84.SUTTON CEMETERY (A-1)
        Located on SR 1302, .7 mile NW of the junction with SR 1308,
        on the SW side of the road, .2 mile in a field.

Thomas William Sutton : 12 Jul 1858 - 21 Dec 1948

Margaret C. Futtrell, wife of T.W. Sutton, Jr. : 1 Dec 1858 - 22 Feb 1919

Lewis M. Sutton, son of T.W. & M. Sutton : 24 Apr 1895 - 30 Aug 1900

Wm. Ben Sutton : 24 Apr 1899 - 21 Oct 1933

P.B. Hobbs : 9 Feb 1856 - 18 Jan 1923

J. Harvey Sutton : 5 Jun 1888 - 11 Jun 1940

85. HOLLOMAN CEMETERY (B-1)
    Located on SR 1006, .3 mile west of the junction with US 117 BY PASS, on the south side of the road, .1 mile in a field.

Elisha J. Coley : 22 Aug 1904 - 2 Sep 1905

Virginia Thompson, dau. of J.T. & Jennie Thompson :
    7 Dec 1904 - 17 Jan 1905

Lizzie Holloman : 2 Jul 1903 -   ?

[There were eight homemade markers here that were unreadable]

86. REGISTER CEMETERY (A-4)
    Located on SR 1301, .6 mile north of the junction with SR 1338, .1 mile on the west side of the road, in a field.

Matilda P., wife of M.J. Waters : 7 Jun 1837 - 17 Feb 1879, Mother

Olivia Register : Died 25 Mar 1876, Aged 65 years, Grandmother

87. BOWDEN CEMETERY (A-4)
    Located on SR 1338, .6 mile west of US 117, (Bowdens), on the north side of the road.

Richard P. Poythress : 18 Oct 1871 - 20 Mar 1947
    same stone
Laura B. : 15 Oct 1872 - 31 May 1958

Heppie E. Jerman, wife of Benjamin Bowden : 12 Apr 1847 - 14 Sep 1915

Benjamin Christopher Bowden : 9 Feb 1821 - 6 Jun 1901

Mary Louise Bowden, dau. of B.C. & H.E. Bowden :
    16 Jan 1881 - 6 Feb 1881

Morehead Bowden, son of Daniel & Edney Bowden :
    10 Apr 1858 - 18 Mar 1860

John F. Bowden, son of Daniel & Edney A. Bowden :
    6 Sep 1855 - [stone buried]

[Several other unmarked graves]

88. BELL CEMETERY (E-3)
    Located on SR 1306, .8 mile east of the intersection with SR 1004, on the north side of the road.

Nathan H. Bell : 1 Feb 1875 - 1 Sep 1926
    same stone
Maude D. : 30 May 1875 - 27 Jul 1944

54

Peggy Sue Bell, dau. of Elmore E. & Rosa B. Bell : 14 Jan 1947

Scott W. Bell : 27 Jan 1907 - 4 Jun 1908

Rossie Bell : 27 Jan 1912 - 7 Nov 1915

Latha Jones, wife of Elias Bell : 20 Apr 1850 - 9 Sep 1922

Elias Bell : 18 Mar 1830 - 29 Aug 1903

Scott Bell : 24 Jun 1873 - 7 Jun 1908

Sarah Kornegay, wife of Aja Jones : 28 Feb 1851 - 26 Oct 1934

Aga Jones : 27 Mar 1848 - 3 Jan 1914

Burtie Herring, wife of Willie Outlaw : 5 Feb 1893 - 21 Aug 1911

Infant son of W. & B. Outlaw : b. & d. 20 Aug 1911

Giles Sutton : 13 Mar 1844 - 28 May 1917

William Taylor, CO A 38 NC INF CSA

89. DAIL CEMETERY (E-3)
    Located on SR 1306, 1.1 miles east of the intersection with SR 1004,
    on the north side of the road.

Claude Dail : 4 Sep 1877 - 8 Jan 1964, Father
    same stone
Loney B. : 2 Sep 1877 - 15 Nov 1954, Mother

Forrest Dail : 22 Nov 1909 - 7 Dec 1967, Daddy
    same stone
Lela Swinson : 23 Nov 1910 - n.d.

90. GARNER CEMETERY (E-3)
    Located on SR 1306, 1.3 miles east of the intersection with SR 1004,
    .1 mile on the north side of the road.

Johnnie Wilbert Bell : 5 Jul 1917 - 17 Oct 1963
    same stone
Retha M. Jones : 22 Mar 1923 - n.d.

Math Bell : 19 Apr 1880 - 1 Jan 1951
    same stone
Carrie Bennett : 22 Nov 1885 - 4 Jun 1964

MM unreadable

Haywood Baines Dail, son of Erastus & Daisy Dail :
    26 Nov 1932 - 17 May 1933

[Dora Bessie, wife of Zeb Garner : 7 Oct 1887 - 7 Jul 1919]

Zeb V. Garner : 1 Jan 1878 - 19 Feb 1949
    same stone
Cora Bessie : 7 Oct 1887 - 7 Jul 1919

Mollie, wife of John Bennett : 27 Mar 1861 - 10 Jun 1935

James B. Bennett : 16 Dec 1889 - 2 Apr 1920

John H. Bennett : 9 Aug 1847 - 15 Sep 1904

Walter M. Dail : 17 Nov 1872 - 16 Dec 1956
    same stone
Glennie : 24 Apr 1878 - 3 May 1951

MM unreadable

Isaac Webster Garner : 25 Nov 1931 - n.d., NC PVT 65 SPRUCE SQ.

Marion Franklin Garner : 25 Aug 1893 - 21 Dec 1917

Simeon Garner : 17 Apr 1851 - 23 Nov 1923

Sarah, wife of S. Garner : 14 Feb 1865 - 19 Mar 1908

Vina Dail, wife of Jeff Garner : 26 Nov 1890 - 25 Jul 1920

Jeff Garner : 14 May 1884 - 12 May 1955

Annie S. Garner : 5 Sep 1902 - 5 Feb 1977

Morris "Wheeler" Garner : 31 Mar 1913 - 13 Aug 1979

B.A. Mincy : 15 Dec 1869 - 17 Jun 1925

Martha Jones Mincey : 13 Dec 1870 - 11 Jun 1928

Margie Ruth Mincey : 12 Apr 1922 - 18 Oct 1923

Ben Frank Mincey : 9 Oct 1894 - n.d.
    same stone
Mary Sue : 9 May 1896 - 5 Feb 1957

Moses Daniel Garner : 21 Nov 1912 - 16 Jul 1962
    same stone
Lottie H. : 23 Apr 1921 - n.d.

91. WILKINS CEMETERY (E-3)
    Located on SR 1507, .6 mile south of the junction with SR 1506,
    .3 mile on the east side of the road in a clearing in the woods.

Bradley Wilkins :   13 Aug 1879 - 8 May 1957

Louvenia Wilkins :   1850 - 13 Aug 1915

H. [T.] Wilkins :   29 Feb 1852 - 9 Nov 1926

Two MM, unreadable

Florie Ann Dail :   27 Dec 1939 - [4 Jan 1939?]

Baby Dail :   10 Jul 1937 - 10 Jul 1937

Baby Dail :   b. & d. 8 Jun 1935

Mary Ruth Dail :   14 Jan 1934 - 14 Jul 1934

Lula M, wife of Dobson Dail :   7 Feb 1905 - 25 May 1951

Dobson Dail :   13 Jul 1902 - 22 Oct 1983, MM

Cassie Dail Wilkins, dau. of Charley & Sarah Wilkins :
    11 Aug 1905 - 24 Nov 1925

Edward A. Dail, son of Dobson & Cassie Dail : 6 Oct 1925 - 10 Mar 1926

Mary Ellen Wilkins :   22 Dec 1897 - 8 Apr 1929

Patsy, wife of Frank Wilkins : 19 Jun 1869 - 4 Feb 1926

B. Frank Wilkins :   31 Aug 1879 - 21 Oct 1951

Vivie H. Wilkins :   11 Oct 1896 - 7 Feb 1971

Franklin D. Wilkins, son of Frank & Vivie Wilkins :
    26 Jan 1934 - 25 Sep 1934

MM unreadable

Pearl C. Sutton :   4 Jul 1904 - 28 Aug 1947

Emmett Wilkins :   20 Apr 1899 - 22 Jan 1929

Ben Frank Wilkins, son of Emmett & Pearl Wilkins :
    9 Jun 1924 - 8 Jul 1924

Infant of Emmett & Pearl Wilkins : b. & d. 11 May 1921

Clarence Sutton :   Aug 1947 [Age unreadable], MM

92. McGOWEN CEMETERY (F-4)
        Located on SR 1300, 1.2 miles east of the intersection with SR 1004,
        .5 mile on the north side of the road in the woods on a logging road.

Joseph McGowen : 20 Jul 1783 - 3 Jul 1851

Hannah Green, wife of Joseph McGowen : 10 Mar 1790 - 13 Oct 1854

93. WILLIAMSON CEMETERY (F-4)
        Located on SR 1300, 1 mile north of the junction with SR 1516,
        in a field.

Pitt Williamson : 11 Apr 1883 - 22 Oct 1920

[Cemetery was grown over, no other stones evident]

94. BRINSON CEMETERY (O-1)
        Located on NC 50, .6 mile south of the intersection with SR 1959,
        on the east side of the road.

Cora Bostic Brinson, wife of Amos J. Brinson :
        2 Sep 1887 - 28 Mar 1964

Amos J. Brinson : 23 Dec 1877 - 8 Aug 1930

Eleanor Louise Brinson, dau. of A.J. & Cora Brinson :
        30 Aug 1925 - 10 Apr 1926

Infant dau. of Cora & A.J. Brinson : 15 Sep 1921

Infant son of Cora & A.J. Brinson : 29 Mar 1927

Hiram J. Brinson : 7 May 1851 - 12 Mar 1936

Irene, wife of H.J. Brinson : 29 Jan 1851 - 26 Apr 1915

Annie Irene Brinson, dau. of A.G. & F.A. Brinson :
        1 Apr 1917 - 31 Jul 1917

Florence A., wife of A.G. Brinson : 31 Aug 1888 - 12 Jul 1917

Ashley G. Brinson : 18 Mar 1887 - 23 Jul 1961, Husband
        same stone
Mary E. : 21 Apr 1902 - n.d., Married 15 Dec 1924, Wife

Leroy H. Brinson : 17 May 1890 - 28 Jun 1947

Infant son of L.H. & Eva Brinson : 18 Aug 1927

Infant son of J.B. & Emma Brinson : 22 Jun 1932

Infant son of J.B. & Emma Brinson : 21 Jun 1929

Jesse B. Brinson : 11 Mar 1873 - 1 Dec 1948, Father

95. BLANCHARD CEMETERY (R-4)
    Located on SR 1970, 1 mile north of the junction with SR 1827,
    on the east side of the road.

Zachariah Blanchard : 18 Feb 1848 - 26 Feb 1920

Bettie Blanchard : 19 Mar 1858 - 5 Apr 1917

Norwood Pitt Blanchard : 6 Dec 1903 - n.d.
    same stone
Mattie Gaylor Blanchard : 6 Feb 1902 - 25 Mar 1976

Doris S. Blanchard : 1 Jul 1940 - 29 Jun 1978

Wyatt Zachariah Blanchard, son of Zachariah & Bettie Blanchard :
    26 Sep 1891 - 14 Dec 1900

Maury R. Blanchard, son of Zachariah & Betty Blanchard :
    23 Oct 1898 - 13 Jul 1908

96. PICKETT CEMETERY (Q-4)
    Located on SR 1970, .7 mile north of the junction with SR 1827,
    on the west side of the road.

Hester Pickett : 20 May 1796 - 28 Jun 1864, Mother

William Pickett : 19 Jan 1763 - 5 Oct 1840

97. GRADY MEMORIAL MARKER (H-4)
    Located on NC 11, about 10 miles north of Kenansville, on
    the grounds of B.F. Grady Elementary School.

John Grady
1703-1787

Mary Whitfield, his wife

"Original settlers lived
and buried near this spot"

Children

William	Mary
Alexander	Charity
Lewis	Anne
Frederick	Elizabeth
John, Jr.	Margaret
Mrs. Wm. Grady Laws	

[This memorial marker is of the same design as the James Outlaw Marker]

98. CHARLES KORNEGAY CEMETERY (G-3)
    Located on SR 1501, .5 mile north of the intersection with SR 1519,
    .5 mile east in a field.

Sarah A., wife of C.J. Kornegay : 9 Sep 1856 - 17 Oct 1918

Charles J. Kornegay : 27 Jun 1855 - 9 Apr 1924

Henry R. Kornegay, son of Charles J. & Sarah A. Kornegay :
    18 Apr 1881 - 12 Feb 1882

Henry R. Kornegay : 26 May 1823 - 4 Feb 1898
    *[Father of Charles J.,Bob & Fisher Kornegay]

Wooden marker, unreadable

Haywood Glisson : 16 Jun 1812 - 13 Mar 1890

Susan Linda Glisson : 6 Sep 1826 - 30 Apr 1895, Mother

Sarah, wife of George F. Kornegay, Sr. :
    24 Feb 1791 - 28 Apr 1859

Mary A.G. Kornegay, dau. of Rev. Henry R. & Jennette Kornegay :
    22 Apr 1848 - 19 Oct 1867

Jennette, wife of Rev. Henry R. Kornegay : 2 Jul 1824 - 10 Sep 1868

Mary Green Kornegay, dau. of Abram & Lucy Kornegay :
    Died 16 Jul 1875, Age 17 years - Erected by Wade H. Kornegay, 1904

*[Information from Mr. Harold Kornegay]

99. CARTER CEMETERY (B-4)
    Located on SR 1301, .5 mile west of the junction with SR 1346,
    .3 mile south of the road in a field.

Infant son of Benson & Lottie C. Holland : 2 Feb 1945

William Alsie Carter : 28 Sep 1875 - 24 Jul 1949
    same stone
Kathleen Carter Herring : 29 Aug 1904 - n.d.

Mabel Carter Tyndall - 9 May 1943 - 9 Aug 1981, Daughter

Charlie Herbert Carter : 1905 - 1973, MM

MM unreadable

100. CHERRY CEMETERY (D-2)
    Located on SR 1004, .7 mile NW of the junction with SR 1504,
    .6 mile SW in a field.

Finnie Talamage Cherry : 29 Aug 1897 - 26 Mar 1945

Dorothy May Cherry : 4 May 1935 – 26 Nov 1935

Mattie Ruth Cherry : 21 May 1930 – 21 Jan 1933

George Washington Cherry : 15 Mar 1870 – 3 Jun 1951
    same stone
Ruth Meeks Cherry, his wife : 12 May 1874 – 14 Sep 1924

Callie Cherry, dau. of G.W. & Ruth Cherry : 1900 – 1908

Willie Cherry, son of G.W. & Ruth Cherry : 1897 – 1901

MM unreadable

Lottie Ruth Cherry : 18 Jan 1928 – 14 May 1929

Elbert Romy Cherry : 29 Apr 1905 – 28 Jul 1956

Lemuel Cherry : 29 Apr 1839 – 12 Feb 1915
    same stone
Ellen Cherry, his wife : 10 Nov 1843 – 12 Mar 1913

William D. Cherry : 20 Jun 1875 – 10 Apr 1946
    same stone
Mary J. Cherry : 5 Mar 1879 – 15 May 1970

Jim Cherry : 22 Feb 1875 – 16 Jun 1947

Willis D. Cherry : CORP CO E 20 NC INF CSA

MM unreadable

Andrew Franklin Cherry : 12 Sep 1865 – 26 Nov 1936
    same stone
Margaret Ann : 9 Apr 1860 – 20 Jan 1935

101. MORTON CEMETERY (D-5)
    Located .2 mile north of the junction of SR 1378 and SR 1377,
    in a field.

William H. Morton : 20 Oct 1840 – 5 Jul 1904, CO B 24 REGT NC TROOPS CSA
MM unreadable

102. BETHANY CHURCH CEMETERY (H-3)
    Located on NC 111, .1 mile north of the junction with SR 1555,
    on the east side of the road.

Eula Mae Herring : 17 Oct 1949 – 13 Oct 1972

Samuel U. Herring : 24 Apr 1889 – 13 Jan 1955, Father
    same stone
Ada Grady : 1 Sep 1896 – n.d.

Dora G. Waters : 21 Apr 1881 – 18 Feb 1964

5. JONES-HARPER CEMETERY (I-2)
  Located on SR 1539, .3 mile SW of the junction with SR 1540,
  .1 mile south of the road on a dirt path. (In two distinct sections).

[Jones section]

Infant of Andrew & Ludia Jones : b. & d. 13 Oct 1918

Andrew F. Jones : 24 Feb 1898 - n.d., Husband
    same stone
Ludia W. Jones : 14 Apr 1896 - n.d., Wife

Leonard H. Jones : 5 Nov 1925 - 17 Jun 1966, Father
    same stone
Louise C. : 27 Nov 1928 - n.d., Mother

N. Franklin Jones : 3 Dec 1906 - 19 Jan 1946, Father
    same stone
Pearl H. : 26 Dec 1904 - 14 Apr 1976, Mother

Lewis Nelson Jones : 28 Jan 1879 - 19 Feb 1947, Father
    same stone
Sarah Winnifred Jones : 2 Feb 1880 - 25 Feb 1948, Mother

Albert M. Wiley : 24 May 1905 - n.d.
    same stone
Myrtle J. : 10 Feb 1905 - 23 Mar 1977, Mama

James A. Jones : 3 Mar 1900 - n.d.
    same stone
Lou Ellen H. : 11 Oct 1906 - n.d.

Lewis H. Jones : 25 Aug 1928 - 15 Mar 1962

Johnny T. Jones : 30 Oct 1882 - 23 May 1953

Randy D. Hill : 28 Jul 1955 - 14 Aug 1971

Major W. Jones : 26 Dec 1911 - 18 Feb 1983, Daddy

[Harper section]

Mattie Sue Parker : 1901 - 1947

Larry Elton Mize : 1944 - 1944

Carolyn Faye Sullivan, dau. of Mr. & Mrs. William Sullivan :
    12 Jul 1943 - 13 Jul 1943

Cena Harper Herring : 2 Apr 1893 - 19 Nov 1965

James Allen Harper : 18 Oct 1855 - 11 Feb 1941

Julia Ann, wife of James A. Harper : 30 Oct 1852 - 6 Dec 1929

Bessie South Jenkins : 3 Feb 1925 - 12 Nov 1964

Betty S. Harper : 16 Dec 1930 - 2 Sep 1979

Herbert Allen Harper : 25 Aug 1947 - 19 Sep 1961

Arlene Lee, wife of Felix Harper : 8 Jan 1924 - 1 May 1977

Tesia C. Harper, dau. of Luba & Lola Harper : 27 Aug 1912 - 2 May 1913

Luby Harper, Jr., son of Luby & Lola Harper : 11 Dec 1933 - 16 Dec 1933

Sammie Harper : 21 Jun 1914 - 24 Jul 1939

Luby Harper : 5 Nov 1884 - 15 Jan 1972
        same stone
Lola Thompson : 9 Apr 1888 - 25 Apr 1970

104. FAISON CEMETERY (C-3)
        Located on SR 1304, .4 mile SE of the junction with SR 1354,
        .4 mile east of the road on a farm road, north side in a field.

    William W. Faison : 1 May 1810 - 13 Mar 1868

    Lilias Serena Faison, dau. of William W. & Elizabeth Faison :
        4 Jul 1854 - 15 Jul 1855

105. GRANT CEMETERY (C-3)
        Located on SR 1354, .3 mile west from the junction with SR 1304,
        on the north side of the road.

    Oscar C. Grant, son of Stafford & Margaret C. Grant :
        25 Mar 1869 - 28 Oct 1918, [Woodman of the World marker]

    Margaret C. Dobson, wife of Stafford Grant : 17 May 1849 - 30 Aug 1917

    Belle Grant, dau. of Stafford & Margaret C. Grant : 25 Jan 1885 - 8 Jun 191

106. BENNETT CEMETERY (A-3)
        Located on SR 1337, .5 mile west of the junction with US 117,
        .4 mile north of the road at the end of a farm road, in a field.

    Susan, wife of Sam Anderson : 31 May 1858 - 1 Aug 1911

    John A. Bennett : 3 Apr 1866 - 16 Mar 1913

    Easter Emmalina Bennett : 1 Jun 1828 - 18 Mar 1908

107. HOOKS CEMETERY (C-3)
        Located on SR 1304, .4 mile SE of the junction with SR 1354,
        .5 mile east of the road on a farm road, south side in edge of woods.

    Eliza Jane Hatch & babe; dau. of Charles & Ann Hooks : 9 Dec 1799 - 9 Oct 1

3. HARDY CEMETERY   -(C-3)
   Located on SR 1358, .3 mile west of the junction with SR 1305,
   .3 mile on the north side of the road, in the woods.

Charity Hardy :   10 Mar 1856 - 22 Oct 1924, Sister

Catharine, wife of A.J. Hardy :   30 Mar 1822 - 16 Jan 1899

Andrew J. Hardy :   13 Feb 1821 - 1 Sep 1894

Phineas Hardy, son of A.J. & Catharine Hardy : 23 May 1850 - 11 Dec 1896

John H. Hardy, son of A.J. & Catharine Hardy : 2 Dec 1864 - 10 Mar 1927

Egbert Hardy, son of A.J. & Catharine Hardy : 19 Apr 1852 - 8 Jul 1933

Ira T. Hardy, son of A.J. & Catharine Hardy : 12 Feb 1854 - 12 Jan 1928

William Christopher Kalmar : 7 Oct 1921 - 19 Dec 1974
   M SGT US ARMY WWII

John Nicholas Kalmar :   14 Aug 1928 - 1 Jan 1982, US ARMY KOREA

9. ROOTY BRANCH FREE WILL BAPTIST CHURCH CEMETERY (E-3)
   Located on SR 1306, .4 mile west of the intersection with SR 1004,
   on the north side of the road.

Yancy Rogers :   29 Apr 1863 - 3 Apr 1940
   same stone
Hattie :   29 Aug 1891 - 9 Dec 1915

Tony Lee Rogers :   14 May 1965 - 16 May 1965

Giles Rodgers :   19 Oct 1829 - 29 Mar 1922

Nancy, wife of Giles Rogers :   1833 - 1 May 1926

Jimmie Rodgers :   8 May 1911 - 29 Jul 1928

Margaret Rogers :   1876 - 1960

Frank Rogers :   1905 - 1971

Infant son of Ransom & Clarice Ezzell : 2 May 1920 - 22 May 1920

Infant son of Ransom & Clarice Ezzell : 9 Dec 1923 - 9 Dec 1923

Clarice E., wife of Ransom Ezzell : 2 Feb 1882 - 11 Dec 1923

Sallie J. Taylor, wife of George Blalock : 17 Jul 1884 - 8 Sep 1962

Charlotte Elizabeth, wife of Rev. L.C. Taylor :   1857 - 1929

Rev. L.C. Taylor : 5 Apr 1854 - 17 Apr 1927

Oliver Jones : 4 May 1855 - 14 Jun 1927
      same stone
Lillie C. Jones : 15 Dec 1872 - 21 Jun 1932

Jessie Westbrook, Jr., son of Jessie & Mollie Westbrook :
      25 May 1933 - 8 Jan 1935

Gilbert Jones, son of F.A. & Dora Jones : 10 Nov 1913 - 4 Jan 1921

Furney A. Jones : 12 Sep 1866 - 19 Sep 1941, Father
      same stone
Dora : 11 Nov 1876 - 19 May 1925, Mother

Alonzo Jones : 1878 - 1949
      same stone
Julia : 1885 - n.d.

MM unreadable

Mable Outlaw Goodman : 8 Feb 1901 - 10 Oct 1918
      same stone
Foye Goodman : 15 Apr 1893 - 4 Apr 1959, Husband
      same stone
Nettie Brown Goodman : 16 Dec 1904 - 16 Dec 1971, Wife

Infant of Foye & Nettie Goodman : b. & d. 1 Feb 1924

Infant son of Foye & Nettie Goodman : 17 Sep 1939

Foye Goodman, Jr., son of Foye & Nettie Goodman :
      8 Feb 1925 - 19 Feb 1925

Christine Goodman, dau. of Foye & Nettie Goodman :
      31 May 1926 - 6 Jul 1926

Henry Preston Chestnutt : 13 Sep 1870 - 24 Jul 1955
      same stone
Lissie Bell Chestnutt : 28 Nov 1870 - 14 May 1944

Harriett Goodman Chestnutt : 19 Sep 1900 - 29 May 1981
      same stone
Daniel James Chestnutt : 1 Mar 1900 - 6 Oct 1969

Eunice Chestnutt, dau. of D.J. & Harriett Chestnutt :
      20 Jul 1927 - 27 Sep 1927

Scott Chestnutt, son of D.J. & Herritte Chestnutt : b. & d. 5 Aug 1925

Russell Dean Jones : 1 Aug 1952 - 27 Dec 1952, Baby

Enos D. Jones : 23 Oct 1889 - 20 Jul 1936
      same stone
Hadie, his wife : 5 May 1896 - 3 Dec 1965

Daniel Edward Jones : 8 Jun 1930 - 16 Jun 1930, Baby

Zular Jones, dau. of Enous D. & Haddie Jones : 14 Dec 1917 - 21 May 1919

George Robert Goodman : 7 May 1856 - 8 Aug 1937, Father
     same stone
Ann Eliza Goodman, his wife : 16 Aug 1861 - 30 Jun 1932, Mother

Loys Green : 17 Feb 1914 - 14 Apr 1982, PFC US ARMY WWII

John H. Summerlin : 1 Apr 1865 - 12 Feb 1928

Henry Preston Vernon : 26 May 1914 - 1 Jun 1979, US ARMY WWII

Myrtie S. Winders : 20 Sep 1877 - 13 Nov 1960

Two MM, unreadable

John T. Howard : 27 Jul 1840 - 7 Jul 1921

Nancy Summerlin : 1876 - 1953
     same stone
Floyd Summerlin : 1880 - 1961

Debbie Jean Summerlin : 11 Feb 1960 - 1 Feb 1965

Two MM, unreadable

Mary S. Summerlin : Died 31 Mar 1961, Age 82, MM

John L. Summerlin : 25 Nov 1873 - 25 Oct 1938
     same stone
Dealie R. : 22 Jun 1877 - 11 Jan 1943

Ebbert Summerlin : 22 Sep 1918 - 10 Aug 1919

Edna M. Summerlin, dau. of E.J. & Lucy Summerlin :
    21 Mar 1921 - 14 Sep 1921

Lacy Summerlin, son of E.J. & Lucy Summerlin :
    4 Aug 1929 - 28 Feb 1931

Edgar J. Summerlin : 22 May 1893 - 13 Oct 1963, Father, NC PFC US ARMY WWII
     same stone
Lucy L. Summerlin : 20 Jan 1897 - 26 Apr 1981, Mother

John Burton Pate, son of Willard & Emma Louis Pate :
    19 Nov 1932 - 17 Jun 1934

John Willard Pate : 12 Nov 1911 - 11 Dec 1962, NC CPL HQ 4266 QM SER BN WWII
     same stone
Emma Louis : 4 Jul 1910 - n.d.

Addie Jones, wife of Herbert J. Summerlin : 16 Dec 1900 – 15 Jan 1936
    same stone
Herbert J. Summerlin : 17 Mar 1895 – 30 Sep 1964
   NC BUGLER CO C 321 INF WWII
    same stone
Lannie Ezzell, wife of Herbert J. Summerlin : 1 Jan 1919 – n.d.

Lewis J. Summerlin : 13 Feb 1867 – 2 Dec 1945
    same stone
Emma D. : 15 Mar 1871 – 17 Jun 1953

Edwin L Vernon : 1 Nov 1890 – 22 Jul 1966

Melvin Gray Vernon, son of E.L. & M.K. Vernon : 19 Nov 1923 – 9 Feb 1940

Maude A. Vernon : 4 Feb 1890 – 10 Aug 1970

Three MM, unreadable

Ella J. Herring : 31 Jul 1891 – 1 Dec 1970

Annie E. Herring : 3 Apr 1869 – 2 Feb 1934

Roland O. Turner : 15 May 1900 – 26 Oct 1958, Father
    same stone
Pearl J. : 5 Feb 1903 – 21 Mar 1933, Mother

MM unreadable

Freddie J. Price : 3 Sep 1901 – 24 Jan 1941
    same stone
Mary Bell : 23 Feb 1903 – n.d.

Isadora Bell : 21 Sep 1907 – 21 Aug 1949
    same stone
Lem A. Bell : 21 Oct 1907 – 17 Feb 1959

110. HARDY CEMETERY (H-1)
        Located on N.C. 903,.9 mile north of the intersection with SR 1306,
        .1 mile on the east side of the road; behind another Hardy cemetery
        previously recorded in DUPLIN COUNTY CEMETERY RECORDS Vol. A, page 8.

Herman Hardy, son of Alonzo & Ellen Hardy : 14 Oct 1918 – 29 Nov 1937

Elender Hardy, dau. of Alonzo & Ellen Hardy : 1 Dec 1916 – 30 Apr 1918

Alonzo Hardy, Jr., son of Alonzo & Ellen Hardy :
    20 Mar 1925 – 1 Dec 1925

Jesse Hardy : 7 Oct 1826 – 31 Oct 1881

Sarah Worley, wife of Jesse Hardy : Died 15 Sep 1919, Age 70

HERRING CEMETERY (G-3)
    Located on SR 1519, .2 mile east of the intersection with SR 1306,
    .1 mile east of the road in a field. [To be relocated in the
    Mt. Olive Cemetery, Mt. Olive, NC.]

Benjamin F. Herring : 17 Aug 1864 - 25 Apr 1932, Father
    same stone
Abba E. : 30 Apr 1878 - 8 Mar 1951, Mother

Bertha Herring, dau. of Ben & Lizzie Herring : 26 Sep 1900 - 28 Nov 1900

Selma E. Herring Marshburn, dau. of B.F. & Lizzie Herring :
    22 Sep 1918 - 29 Nov 1947

.*WILLIAMS CEMETERY (T-4)
    Located on SR 1826, .2 mile NW of the Duplin/Onslow county line
    where SR 1826 exits the county, in a field.

Jethro A. Horne : 24 Nov 1907 - 16 Oct 1965
    same stone
Viola A. Horne : 7 Oct 1915 - 25 Dec 1973

J. Calvin Batchelor : 13 Apr 1901 - 3 Feb 1972
    same stone
Rosie B. Batchelor : 11 Jun 1923 - n.d.

Infant son of J.C. & Rosa Batchelor : 26 Aug 1953 - 26 Aug 1953

J.C. Batchelor : 27 Oct 1940 - 5 Nov 1940

Walter T. Batchelor : 15 Jun 1923 - 1 Apr 1965

Henry-Mose-Batchelor : 14 Sep 1903 - 1 Dec 1965

Sarah Batchelor : 15 Jun 1899 - 21 Oct 1934

Sallie Batchelor : 26 Aug 1879 - 15 Jun 1949

John E. Williams : 3 May 1856 - 6 Oct 1938

Nancy Jane Williams : 10 Dec 1954 - 18 Dec 1955

Jessie W. Williams : 25 Dec 1893 - 6 Feb 1971

Hettie H. Williams : 14 Mar 1896 - n.d.

S.E. Batchelor : 24 Jul 1873 - 22 Apr 1833

Alf Batchelor : 20 Sep 1843 - 20 Feb 1926

Sarah B. Williams : 13 Jan 1905 - n.d.

Jerry A. Williams : 16 Apr 1903 - 28 Jun 1977

Hughey A. Pearce :   3 Aug 1888 – 19 Feb 1949

Lue Eliza Pearce :   28 Aug 1890 – 18 Aug 1964

Lamuel Holt Williams :   6 May 1863 – 29 Jul 1931

H. Julia Lanier Williams :   2 Jul 1870 – 17 Jun 1925

Two wooden markers, unreadable

Sarah E. Williams, wife of W.W. Brown :   15 Jan 1863 – 23 Mar 1924

Sallie Williams :   1 Oct 1821 – 3 Oct 1908

Lamuel Williams :   Died 20 Apr 1868, Age 80 years

Beulah B. James :   1910 – 1979

Relmond D. James :   1913 – 1980

Perry N. Williams :   26 Apr 1909 – 28 Jan 1938

Florence E. Williams :   6 Oct 1907 – n.d.
  *[From the records of Johnnie D. Manning]

113. *BENJAMIN HORNE CEMETERY (T-4)
          Located on SR 1826, 1 mile SW of the Duplin|Onslow county line
          where SR 1826 exits the county, and about .6 mile west of the road
          on a farm road in a field.

John & Arron Batts :   26 Sep 1970 – 26 Sep 1970

Mary S. Horne :   1898 – n.d.
     same stone
Hosea E. Horne :   1896 – 1983

Mammie B. Horne :   1900 – 1977

Alfred D. Horne :   1895 – 1979

Mary C. Williams :   20 Aug 1884 – 18 Oct 1975

John Wesley Williams :   1872 – 1945

Benjamin A. Horn :   5 Aug 1845 – 18 NOv 1919

Sealie C. Horne :   27 Jul 1856 – 31 Jan 1934

Martha E. Jones :   14 Apr 1880 – 10 Mar 1917

William McKinley Horne :   4 Mar 1906 – 1 Nov 1907

Thaddus L. Horne : 6 Nov 1911 - 7 Oct 1913

Isaac E. Horne : 4 Feb 1916 - 6 Aug 1916

Mattie B. Horn : 6 Sep 1917 - 6 Feb 1918

L.T. Horne : 20 Jul 1875 - 8 Jul 1950

Burras W. Henderson : 3 Jun 1912 - 2 May 1965

Elouise Horne : 9 Feb 1932 - 25 Feb 1932

Mattie B. Horne Brown : 10 Mar 1884 - 16 Nov 1969

Berry Horne : 23 Aug 1878 - 24 Mar 1917

Cornelius Horne : 22 Jan 1862 - 14 Mar 1901

Edward Horne : 17 Jan 1882 - 1 May 1918

Infant of A.D. & Mannie Horne : 9 Aug 1931 - 9 Aug 1931

K.T. Horne : 1878 - 23 Dec 1932

Olive Horne : 8 Sep 1876 - 19 Dec 1950

Roy Horne : Oct 1908 - 1939

Larry E. Brown : 19 Aug 1948 - 9 Sep 1948

Dennie W. Horne : 7 Apr 1905 - 31 Mar 1982

Lindsey Right Horne : 16 Nov 1890 - 23 Apr 1972

Holland J. Horne : 23 May 1893 - 12 Apr 1931

Barbara Horne : 1843 - 1930

Priscilla Williams : 17 Mar 1854 - 16 Oct 1914

H.N. Horne : 18 Jun 1841 - 27 Oct 1926

Perry S. Horne : 18 Sep 1855 - 30 Oct 1930

Emma H. Horne : 13 Oct 1888 - 7 Oct 1974
     same stone
Johnnie N. Horne : 27 Oct 1886 - 13 Jan 1969

Infant dau. of J.R. & Letha Williams : 6 Jul 1936

Major Ellis Williams : 30 Oct 1892 - 22 Aug 1928

Linster Williams : 13 Oct 1885 - 26 Jul 1940

70

Winford L. Brown :   28 Mar 1929 - 29 Mar 1929

Linnie H. Brown :   1 Sep 1900 - 20 Apr 1929

Cyrus J. Brown :   19 Jun 1900 - 19 Jul 1954

Henry L. Horne :   4 Aug 1876 - 12 Nov 1941

Howard Horne :   5 Aug 1925 - 9 Apr 1945

Lonnie Horne :   2 Oct 1889 - 20 Jun 1957

Luther H. Horne :   4 Nov 1891 - 11 May 1960

Thelbert Morris Brown :   7 Nov 1949 - 22 Oct 1978

Teresa Michelle Brown :   1 Jun 1968 - 8 May 1973

*[From the records of Johnnie D. Manning]

114. *BROWN-HOWEL HORNE CEMETERY (T-4)
        Located on SR 1826, 1.7 miles north of the Cypress Creek community
        crossroads, on the west side of the road, .1 mile in a field.

Clyde Brown :   12 Nov 1899 - 3 Jul 1963

Mary Eliza Brown :   12 May 1883 - 19 Jul 1933

Howell Thomas Horne :   3 Feb 1882 - 28 Dec 1974

Watson Horne :   10 Jan 1856 - 24 Feb 1922

Alvania Horne :   6 Sep 1863 - 26 Jul 1934

Clara Horne :   1819 - 24 Jun 1900

Howel Horn :   10 Apr 1822 - 10 Dec 1889

Jacob Brown :   15 Oct 1898 - 30 Dec 1909

Mary E. Brown :   5 Apr 1858 - 12 Jul 1942

J.W. Brown :   15 Dec 1852 - 19 Jun 1930

Stephen Brown :   6 Nov 1881 - 22 May 1929

Seba Brown :   15 Feb 1884 - 23 Dec 1929

*[From the records of Johnnie D. Manning]

115. *MANNING CEMETERY (T-4)
        Located on SR 1826, .8 mile SW of the Duplin/Onslow county line
        from where SR 1826 exits the county; on west side, .2 mile in a field.

Simon Batts :   25 Jul 1903 - 26 Oct 1931

Zeb Thomas Batts :   25 Jul 1903 – 26 Oct 1931

Isabel Batts :   23 Mar 1881 – 16 Aug 1925

Mattie C. Manning Horne : 11 Jan 1888 – 25 Dec 1967

Marten Manning :   22 Aug 1859 – 13 Nov 1940
    same stone
Serena Catherine :   24 Sep 1851 – 22 Feb 1929

Hugh Manning :   30 Sep 1892 – 11 Feb 1929

Sarah A. Manning :   9 Nov 1882 – 22 Jun 1900

Many N. Manning :   1 Jun 1886 – 30 Jun 1898

Merritt Manning :   2 Aug 1890 – 7 Apr 1896

Dunn Manning :   9 Feb 1880 – 30 Apr 1944
    same stone
Piranda Manning :   5 Jul 1891 – 14 Feb 1935

Helen Manning :   27 Oct 1926 – 7 Apr 1927

Sutton Manning :   22 Dec 1920 – 14 May 1921

Neal Manning :   31 Aug 1916 – 2 Apr 1921

Infant son of Dunn & Piranda Manning :   8 Dec 1913

J.W. Horne :   24 Jun 1883 – n.d.
    same stone
Lydia B. Horne :   28 Jan 1884 – 12 Apr 1966

Edwin Horne :   3 Mar 1921 – 16 Mar 1944

Ralph Horne :   5 Dec 1915 – 4 Aug 1921
*[From the records of Johnnie D. Manning]

*MOBLEY-MANNING CEMETERY (T-4)
    Located on SR 1826, .8 mile SW of the Duplin/Onslow county line
    from where SR 1826 exits the county; on the west side of the road.

Two unmarked graves

John L. Manning :   22 Jun 1854 – 7 Jul 1925

Susan J. Manning :   9 Nov 1858 – 18 Nov 1917

Kate Watkins :   18 Feb 1880 – 23 Apr 1963

Lucy J. Mobley :   31 Dec 1849 – 18 Nov 1928

Maxey A. Pickett : 18 Jan 1815 - 20 Dec 1894

Iva L. Mobley : 5 Nov 1877 - 13 Mar 1893

Henry W. Mobley : 2 Aug 1849 - 12 Sep 1911

Nancy C. Mobley : 4 May 1886 - 1 Dec 1900

Williams H. Mobley : 26 Sep 1871 - 19 May 1895

Charles R. Sloan : 15 Nov 1867 - 1 Jan 1947

William R. Swinson : 13 Oct 1908 - 9 Jul 1926

Dicey A. Blake : 8 Feb 1840 - 18 Jun 1924

Charlie E. Swinson : 9 May 1900 - 7 May 1906

Levi C. Swinson : 4 May 1896 - 4 Nov 1903

Alonza E. Swinson : 24 Nov 1897 - 2 Mar 1898

Elizabeth Sloan : 1842 - 28 Jul 1878

Richard R. Swinson : 2 Mar 1876 - 11 Sep 1929

Julia A. Swinson : 22 Dec 1875 - 18 Jan 1959

James G. Swinson : 24 Feb 1917 - 21 Jan 1974

Two wooden marker : [According to Frank Swinson & Albert Manning, John
     S. & Mary Batchelor are buried here.]

*[From the records of Johnnie D. Manning]

117. BLANCHARD CEMETERY (A-6)
     Located on SR 1108, 1.3 miles south of the junction with NC 24,
     (Baltic), .1 mile on the east side of the road, in the woods.

John L. Blanchard : 1823 - 13 Apr 1889

Nancy Drew, wife of John L. Blanchard : 1825 - 25 Apr 1907

Abram Washington Blanchard : 1833 - 10 May 1880

118. HERRING CEMETERY (A-6)
     Located on SR 1108, .7 mile west from the junction with SR 1110,
     on the south side of the road, .2 mile in a field.

Katie C. Herring, dau. of I.W. & R.V. Herring :
     7 May 1879 - 12 Jul 1880

). WILLIAMS CEMETERY (A-6)
   Located on SR 1108, .6 mile west of the junction with SR 1110,
   on the north side of the road, .1 mile in the edge of a field.

A stone marker had the following inscription :

"This cemetery was established by

James K. Williams

& dedicated by wife

Elizabeth E. Williams

under a Duplin County Deed

Recorded in

Deed Book 45 page 39

Placed by

Ruth Williams Alford

10-1-83 "

James K. Williams, son of J.F. & Mary Helen Williams :
   1 Oct 1887 - 8 Jul 1907

Elizabeth Ezzell, wife of James K. Williams :
   13 Sep 1822 - 27 Nov 1900

James K. Williams : Died 23 Oct 1890, Aged 80-0-10

Ellen E. Williams, dau. of James K. & Elizabeth Williams :
   5 Sep 1851 - 28 Jul 1929, Sister

Electra Lestina Williams, dau. of J.K. & Elizabeth A. Williams :
   30 May 1859 - 15 Feb 1930, Sister

Joshua R. Ezzell : 22 Jan 1826 - Died in Service 1865

Patrick Ezzell : 22 Sep 1792 - 2 Mar 1847

Nancy Ezzell : 20 Mar 1802 - 9 Sep 1867

Gladys Kennedy, dau. of J.T. & Lavinia Kennedy :
   1 Jul 1904 - 23 Nov 1904

0. HURST CEMETERY (C-4)
   Located on SR 1351, .2 mile north of the junction with SR 1301,
   .4 mile east of the road, in the edge of the woods.

E.W. Fonvielle, infant son of E.W. & N.S. Fonvielle :
   Died _?_ May 1846, Age [2?]months-2 ? days

Robert K. Hurst : 4 Nov 1839 - 30 Jun 1908, [Masonic emblem]

Mary Jane Collins, wife of James [M.?] Collins :
    Died 8 Aug 1855, Age 19 years

William Hurst : Died 8 Jan 1822, In the 48th year of his age

Margaret Hurst, wife of Williams Hurst : Died 1 Nov 1843,
    In the 62nd year of her age.

Sarah Oliver, wife of Matt Moore : 8 Jul 1833 - 23 Nov 1899

Gertrude H. Moore, dau. of Dr. Matt & Sarah O. Moore :
    24 Feb 1869 - 14 Aug 1919

MM unreadable

121. WRIGHT-LOFTIN CEMETERY (B-4)
        Located on SR 1301, .5 east of the intersection with US 117,
        (Bowden), .4 mile on the north side of the road, in edge of woods.

John Beck Wright : 15 Jan 1798 - 13 Jan 1831

Charity Wright, Consort of James Wright : 5 Dec 1829, Aged 68

James Wright : 5 Dec 1755 - 18 Apr 1840

    [The following were inside a fence, next to the above]
Luther R. Loftin : 31 Aug 1822 - 5 Sep 1865

Susan H. Loftin : 27 Feb 1827 - 4 Dec 1904, wife of L.R. Loftin

Franklin Loftin : 1852 - 1914

David Marion Koonce : 1880 - 1919

Francis Loftin Koonce : 26 Oct 1845 - 15 Feb 1929

Winfield E. Koonce : 1 Nov 1878 - 11 Aug 1932

Oscar Loftin, son of L.R. & Susan Loftin : 15 May 1858 - 29 Sep 1862

Little Martha Loftin, dau. of L.R. & S. Loftin : 21 Mar 1856 - 11 Oct 1857

122. BLOUNT-LOFTIN CEMETERY (B-4)
        Located on SR 1301, 2.2 miles east of the intersection with US 117,
        (Bowden), .1 mile on the south side of the road, in a field.

Samuel P. Blount : 20 Jul 1853 - 30 Jan 1863
    same stone
Julia A. Blount : 26 Aug 1821 - 24 Apr 1866

Dr. J.W. Blount :   12 Jul 1823 - 15 Jul 1903
    same stone
Maria G. Davis, wife of Dr. J.W. Blount : 20 Aug 1823 - 29 Aug 1906

W.S. Loftin :   4 Dec 1847 - 13 Jan 1926
    same stone
Victoria C. Blount, his wife :   26 Oct 1851 - 10 May 1916

Liston L. Loftin, son of W.S. & V.C. Loftin : 29 Dec 1892 - 2 Jul 1895

Susan H. Loftin, dau. of W.S. & V.C. Loftin : 15 Jul 1877 - 19 Apr 1890

Ellanora Loftin, dau. of W.S. & V.C. Loftin : 26 Sep 1872 - 28 Nov 1875

Ernestine Loftin, dau. of W.S. & V.C. Loftin : 18 Oct 1875 - 25 Mar 1877

Fannie V. Loftin, dau. of W.S. & V.C. Loftin : 26 Mar 1879 - Nov 1887

Emma A. Loftin, dau. of W.S. & V.C. Loftin : 8 Oct 1896 - 2 Jul 1911

123. WEEKS CEMETERY (A-4)
    Located on SR 1338, .5 mile west of the junction with SR 1301,
    .3 mile on the north side of the road, up a farm road.

Arthur Weeks :   1 May 1845 - 15 Jun 1911
    same stone
Sarah A. Weeks :   26 Dec 1841 - 21 Jan 1898

124. WILLIAMS CEMETERY (B-3)
    Located on US 117, .8 mile north of Bowden, on the east side of
    the road, in a field.

Daniel D. Harper, son of Daniel & P.J. Harper : 29 Sep 1861 - 10 Sep 1868

Alcy A. Harper : Died 1 Aug 1857, Aged 52-3-11

Redin Croton Williams, son of B.W. & Martha L. Williams :
    17 Jun 1855 - 28 Jul 1855

Eddie Bowden, dau. of B.W. & Martha L. Williams : 11 Dec 1862 - 12 Jun 1864

D.G. Sasser :   Died 29 Jul 1904, Father [no age]

Anna Williams Sasser :   Died 3 Jul 1918, Mother [no age]

Annie Sasser Lee :   Died 15 Jul 1914, Sister [no age]

Martha Lorenza Williams :   Died 11 Jul 1924, Grandmother [no age]

Mollie Louise Williams :   Died 23 Feb 1923 [no age]["Motsey"at the bottom]

125. HENRY GRADY MEMORIAL MARKER* (H-3)
      Located on NC 111 about 1.4 miles north of the junction with
      NC 11, .1 mile off the road on the west side.

[This marker was inscribed on all four sides]

[West Side]

Henry Grady was a

son of Alexander Grady

a son of John Grady, who

married Mary Whitfield

and settled about one mile

south of this spot in 1739.

He was ancestor to all of

the Duplin family of that

name.

[East Side]

Henry Grady
4 Feb 1772 - 31 Aug 1834
and wife

Elizabeth Outlaw Grady
9 May 1774 - 16 Jul 1828

"Erected in 1946
By some of their descendants"

[North Side]

Children

H.P. Grady
12 Jul 1819 - 19 Feb 1820

Clarissa Grady
4 Feb 1803 - 15 Jan 1822

Alexander Outlaw Grady
19 Feb 1800 - 26 Mar 1867

Nancy (Sloan) Grady, his wife
15 Nov 1804 - 16 Jan 1857

Bryan Whitfield Grady
20 Mar 1806 - 12 Dec 1870

Repsy and Patrick H. Grady twins
children by second marriage
28 Jun 1834, died in infancy

[South Side]

Grandchildren

Rachel Elizabeth, dau. of A.O. Grady, 29 Jun 1840 - 1867

Gibson, son of O.A.[sic] Grady, 1835 - 1835

Mary Carolina, dau. of D.H. Simmons, 23 Dec 1835 - 29 Dec 1836

Julia A., dau. of B.W. Grady, 29 Apr 1840 - 5 Feb 1925

Martha, dau. of Harriet Grady Jackson, 1833 - died young

Nancy W., dau. of B.W. Grady, 1849 - 27 May 1935

Margaret Anne, dau. of A.O. Grady, wife of James O'Daniel
6 Jun 1846 - 21 Nov 1901

James O'Daniel, 20 Jun 1844 - 12 May 1912

---

*Recorded by Daniel Fagg. According to him, Romulus O'Daniel, son of
Margaret Grady O'Daniel was buried here (no marker) in the late 1950's
or early 1960's.

126. RITTER CEMETERY   (O-3)
     Located on NC 11, .1 mile south of the junction with SR 1162,
     on the west side of the road, next to a garage.

Charity C. Ritter : 14 May 1845 - 13 May 1926

MM unreadable

Unmarked grave :
     [According to the property owner and local people, this is the
     grave of Ida Ritter, daughter of Charity Ritter. Duplin County
     Death Records show that Ida Pearl Ritter was born on 14 Nov 1885
     and died on 3 Oct 1965, age 80.]

127. GARNER CEMETERY* (F-2)
     Located on SR 1501, .4 mile east of SR 1528, about 1 mile off
     the road up a dirt path on the north side.

Henry Garner : 7 Jan 1825 - 2 Apr 1900

*[From the records of Mrs. V.R. Garner.
Mrs. Garner states that there are at least 12 other unmarked graves
located here, and among them are the graves of Henry Garner's
parents—Nathan Garner and his wife Penelope Kornegay Garner.]

128. BRANCH CEMETERY [WPA]
>   This cemetery is taken from the 1937 WPA Cemetery Records. The
>   only location given was Kenansville, NC

Archelous Branch :   20 Feb 1792 - 18 Apr 1865

Esther Branch :   1785 - 18 May 1841

129. MALLARD CEMETERY [WPA] (P-4)
>   Located on SR 1947, .3 mile SSE from the junction with SR 1948,
>   .3 mile SSW of the road in a field.
>   NOTE : This cemetery has been completely destroyed. There is not
>   any evidence of this cemetery left. The data is from the
>   1937 WPA Cemetery Records and the location is from local
>   citizens.

John Mallard :   1779 - 12 Oct 1854

Barbara Mallard :   22 Dec 1791 - 23 Jul 1860

Dickson Mallard :   1816 - 21 Jan 1877

Mary M. Mallard :   1826 - 1885

Susan Farrior :   26 Jan 1824 - 26 Dec 1854

130. BEASLEY CEMETERY (L-2)
>   Located on SR 1107, .1 mile north of the junction with SR 1104,
>   on the west side of the road, on the E.M. Beasley farm.

Lonnie D. Beasley :   29 Jul 1877 - 26 Mar 1941
     same stone
Mattie C. [Corbett]*Beasley :   13 Mar 1882 - 23 Feb 1952

*According to E.M. Beasley, this was his mother's maiden name; also an
infant daughter of George & Flora Alice Beasley Brooks is buried here.

131. HALL CEMETERY (Q-4)
>   Located on SR 1970, 1.3 miles north of the junction with SR 1827,
>   .2 mile on the west side of the road in edge of the woods.

Infant dau. of S.E. & A.J. Hall :   25 Nov 1889

Ella Thomas Hall :   12 Dec 1883 - 22 Sep 1890

Stephen Edward Hall :   1 Nov 1851 - 12 Feb 1927
     same stone
Asha Chestnut Hall : 26 Sep 1859 - 18 Jan 1912

Martha Helen Hall :   3 Jun 1881 - 22 May 1891

A.J.H. (on footstone)

132. ROUSE CEMETERY (N-2)
>   Located on SR 1911, .2 mile north of the intersection with SR 1912,
>   on the east side of the road, .3 mile off the road at a farm pond.

Joseph S. Rouse : 12 Nov 1847 - 9 Aug 1924, Father
    same stone
Sarah A. Farrier : 7 Aug 1854 - 24 Jul 1919, Mother

Infant son of H.F. & M.D. Rouse : 22 Jun 1925 - 22 Jun 1925

[According to the property owner Mr. Joe Rouse, an old Swinson and Rogers
cemetery is located adjacent to the Rouse cemetery. At one time there
were gravestones, but no evidence exist today - only unreadable wooden
markers and a fence.]

133. CARROLL CEMETERY [Also known as the G.S. Carr Graveyard]   (O-3)
>   Located on NC 11, .4 mile north of the junction with SR 1918, on
>   the west side of the road at the Elder Chapel A.M.E. Zion Church
>   (brick building).

John Carroll : 3 Sep 1770 - 6 Dec 1826

Ann Carroll : 16 Feb 1778 - 16 Jun 1861

134. WELLS-CARR CEMETERY (Supplement)* (N-2)
>   Located on SR 1920, .2 mile south of the junction with SR 1912
>   and SR 1909, about .2 mile off the road on the west side.

*[The readable markers were originally recorded by Leora H. McEachern in
DUPLIN COUNTY GRAVESTONE RECORDS, VOL. 8, page 15. The following data
is from the records of Johnny T. Brown which reveal the names and family
relationships of the individuals buried there with only unreadable wooden
markers at the grave site. This information was passed on to Mr. Brown
by his grandmother - Mora Estelle Carr Brown.]

James Rouse : son of Joe Rouse Sr.

Dollie Wells Rouse : wife of James and daughter of R.D. & Mrs. Wells

Isabel Rouse : 6 months, daughter of Mr. & Mrs. James Rouse

Two Rouse Infants : children of Mr. & Mrs. James Rouse

Raymond Wells : 6 months, son of R.D. & Mrs. Wells

Mac Wells : 14 months, son of R.D. & Mrs. Wells

Two King Infants : sons of George and Maude King

Infant Southerland : child of J.D. & Mary Wells Southerland

135. MIDDLETON CEMETERY   (D-6)
    Located on SR 1376, 1.1 miles east of the junction with NC 24,
    about 200' south of the road.

A.W. Middleton : 3 Sep 1858 - 9 Jun 1916

B.F. Middleton : 31 Dec 1856 - 31 Oct 1910

E.A. Middleton, wife of W.B. Middleton : 26 Sep 1831 - 14 Mar 1909

Wm. B. Middleton : 11 Sep 1824 - 10 Aug 1881 (Masonic emblem)

Mary Delila, dau. of Wm. B. & E.A. Middleton : 5 Oct 1860 - 10 Jul 1861

136. SIMEON and FLORENCE DAIL GARNER CEMETERY (F-2)
    Located on SR 1501, .5 mile east of the junction with SR 1528,
    about .1 mile north of the road behind the Garner-Sloan house.

Simeon Garner : 14 Feb 1866 - 15 Apr 1918

Florence Isedore Dail, wife of Simeon Garner : 31 Oct 1874 - 2 Jun 1972

James C. Garner, son of S. & F.D. Garner : 29 Mar 1912 - 31 Oct 1915

Russell W. Kornegay, son of DeLeon and Sallie M. Kornegay :
    20 Feb 1928 - 29 Dec 1934

Ernest J. Kornegay, son of Sallie & DeLeon Kornegay :
    6 Sep 1925 - 25 Feb 1976

[From the records of Mrs. V.R. Garner]

137. TILLMAN CEMETERY (G-2)
    Located on NC 111, .3 mile NW of the junction with SR 1533, .3 mile
    down path on south side of road.

Bessie Vinson Tillman: 28 Sep 1881 - 28 Apr 1923

Lalar Tillman : 3 Aug 1916 - 4 Sep 1973

Bobby Duncan : Died 1961 (no age given) [husband of Thelma Tillman Duncan]

Norman Tillman : Died 26 Dec 1966 (no age given) MM

[According to Mrs. Thelma Tillman Duncan, property owner and daughter of
 Bessie Vinson Tillman, the following are also buried in this cemetery—
 some with markers without dates and others without any marker]:
    Lula Tillman; Billy Outlaw & Lina Outlaw, brother and sister; Alec
    Tillman, grandfather of Thelma Tillman Duncan; [Mary?] Sutton Outlaw
    Tillman, wife of Alec Tillman; John Tillman, husband of Bessie Vinson
    Tillman & father of Thelma Duncan; Raymond Lane; Lola May Tillman
    Lane, wife of Raymond Lane & sister of Thelma Duncan; John Robert Lane,

infant son of Raymond & Lola May Tillman Lane - died at birth.
[The relationships given were provided by Mrs. Thelma Tillman Duncan]

138.CARR CEMETERY (P-3)
Located on SR 1953, .9 mile NE of the junction with SR 1102, on
the south side of the road, .5 mile off the road in a field.

Infant son of J.D. & Mary W. Carr: 6 Jan 1904 - 10 Jan 1904

Obed W. Murray: 28 Mar 1830 - 4 Mar 1913

Martha L. Carr, wife of Obed W. Murray: 8 Feb 1844 - 29 Jan 1925; Mother

Amanda E. Carr: 13 Feb 1831 - 21 Jul 1913

James Carr: 18 Aug 1797 - 1 Apr 1881
      same stone
Nancy, wife of James Carr: 29 May 1813 - 23 Jan 1897

Jacob David Carr, son of James & Nancy Carr: 5 Oct 1847 - 10 Dec 1847

Sarah Catharine Carr, dau. of J.O. & M.A. Carr: 22 Jan 1881 - 3 Jul 1903

Walter R. Carr: 24 Nov 1867 - 18 Aug 1928; "He was a kind and loving
      son and affectionate brother".

James Owen Carr: 17 Jan 1839 - 1 Jan 1926

Mary Ann Wells, wife of Jas. O. Carr: 21 May 1844 - 27 Feb 1915

139.PHIPPS CEMETERY (C-6)
Located on NC highway 24/50 between Warsaw and Kenansville, .3 mile
west of the junction with SR 1375, about 60' off the road on the
north side in a field.

William H. Phipps: 12 Sep 1824 - 20 May 1903

*[M]elly C., wife of Wm. P. Phipps: 1833 - 7 Jul 1918

    *(This stone was broken, but Duplin County deed book 32 page 744
    indicates that her given name was Milly.)

140. WILLIAMS CEMETERY (D-5)
Located on SR 1301 about .1 mile north of the junction with SR 1398
(P.B. Raiford Airport road), about 75' off road on the west side.

William H. Williams: 22 Apr 1835 - 17 Sep 1889

Mrs. Martha Williams: 25 Sep 1803 - 22 Jan 1875

James Williams: Died 10 Oct 1856, Aged 55 years.

Mrs. Fedorah Williams: Died 27 Jul 1841, Aged 24-7-14

Infant dau. of James & Martha Williams: Died 9 Mar 1847, [no age given]

Harper Williams: Died 25 Oct 1890, Aged 98 years.

Eliza, wife of H.W. Williams: 23 Jun 1818 – 22 Jul 1853

John E., son of Harper & Eliza Williams: 17 Nov 1843 – 10 Sep 1856

    [stone broken at top; given name missing]
...wife of Jas. M. Williams: 30 Aug 1850 – 16 May 1884

[an unearthed footstone in the vicinity of the previous grave has
 the initials "J.N.W."]

James M. Williams, son of Harper & Eliza Williams: 22 Sep 1847 – 14 Dec 1887

DUPLIN COUNTY
NORTH CAROLINA

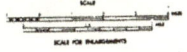

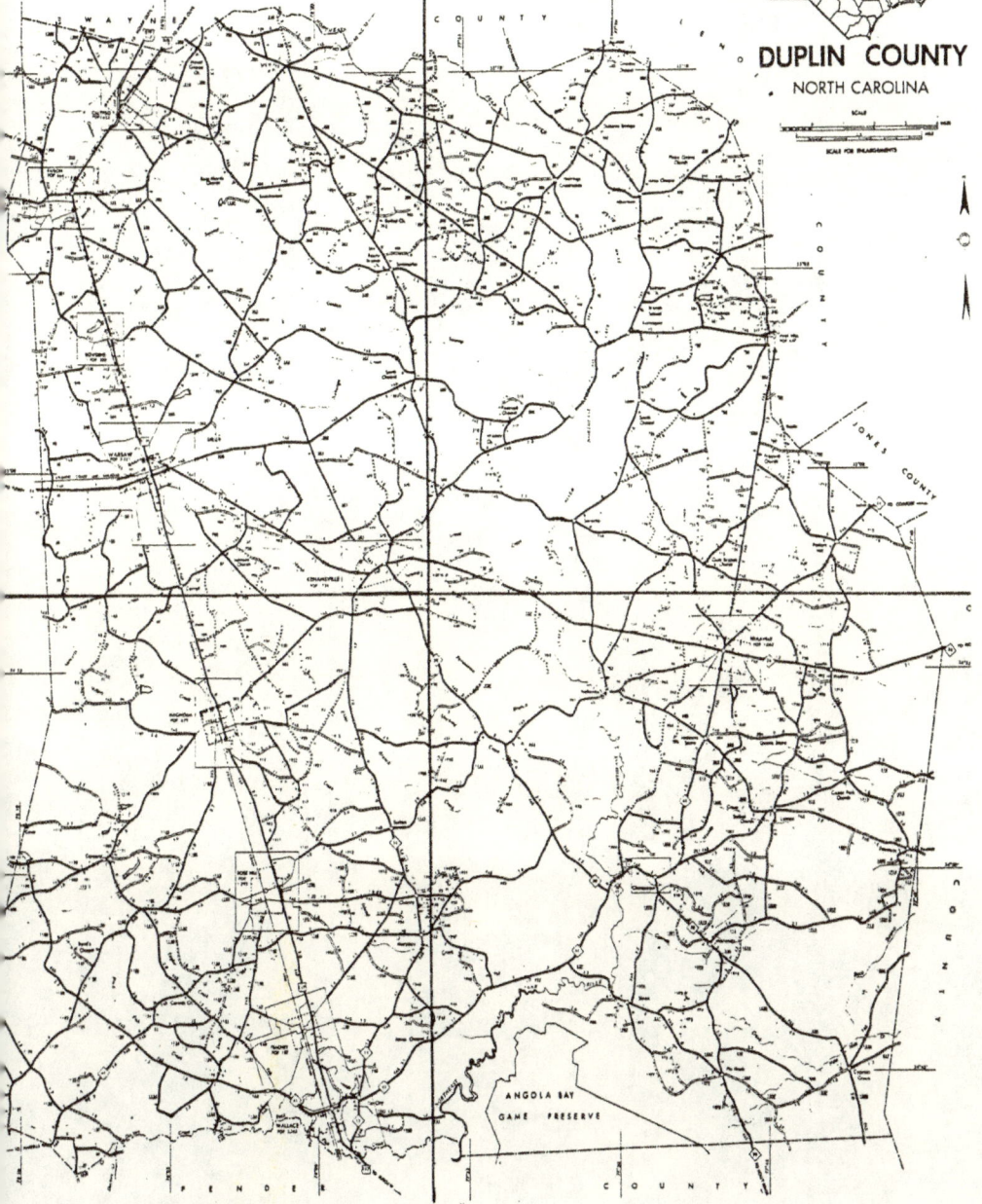

I II III IV

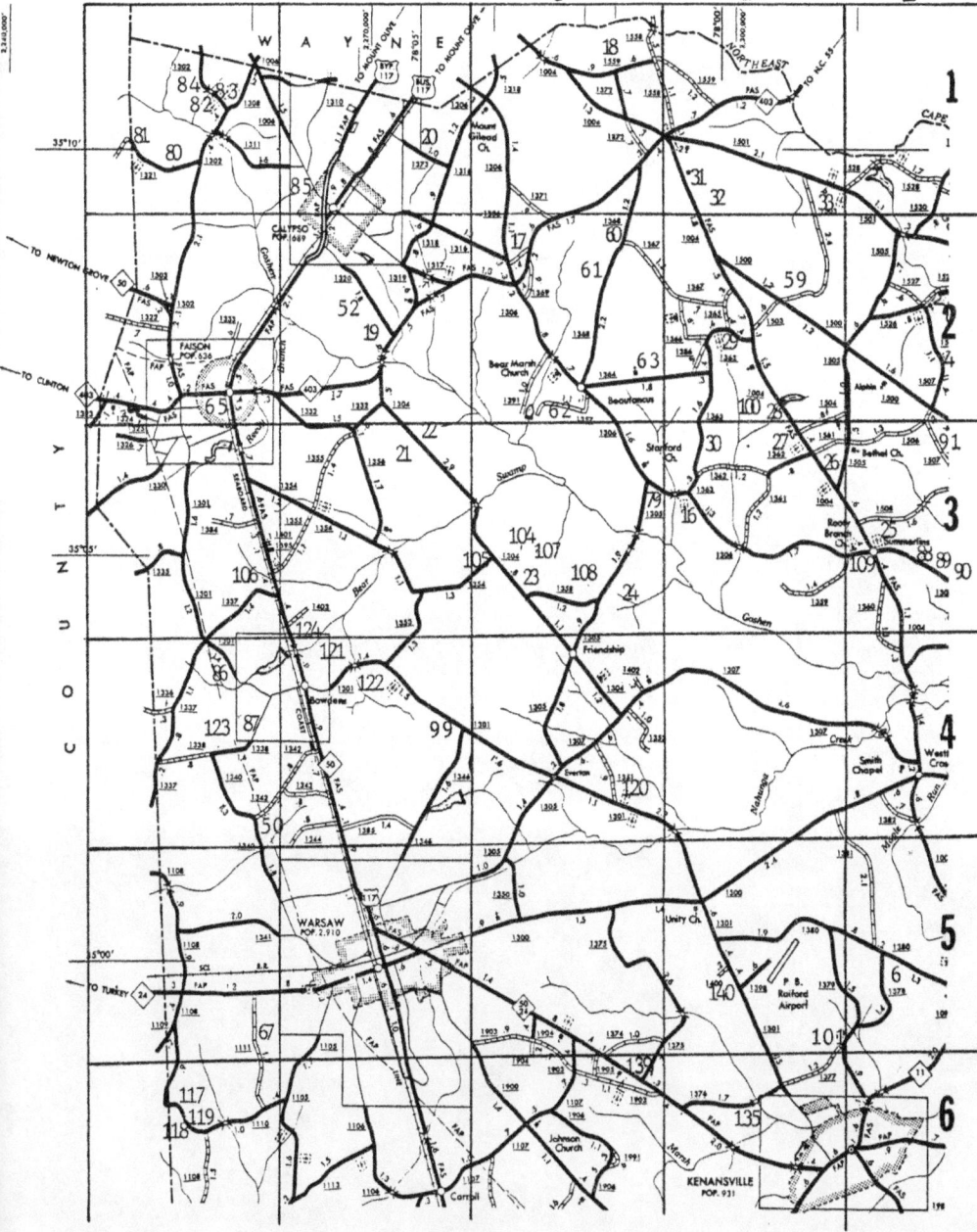

F   G   H   I   J

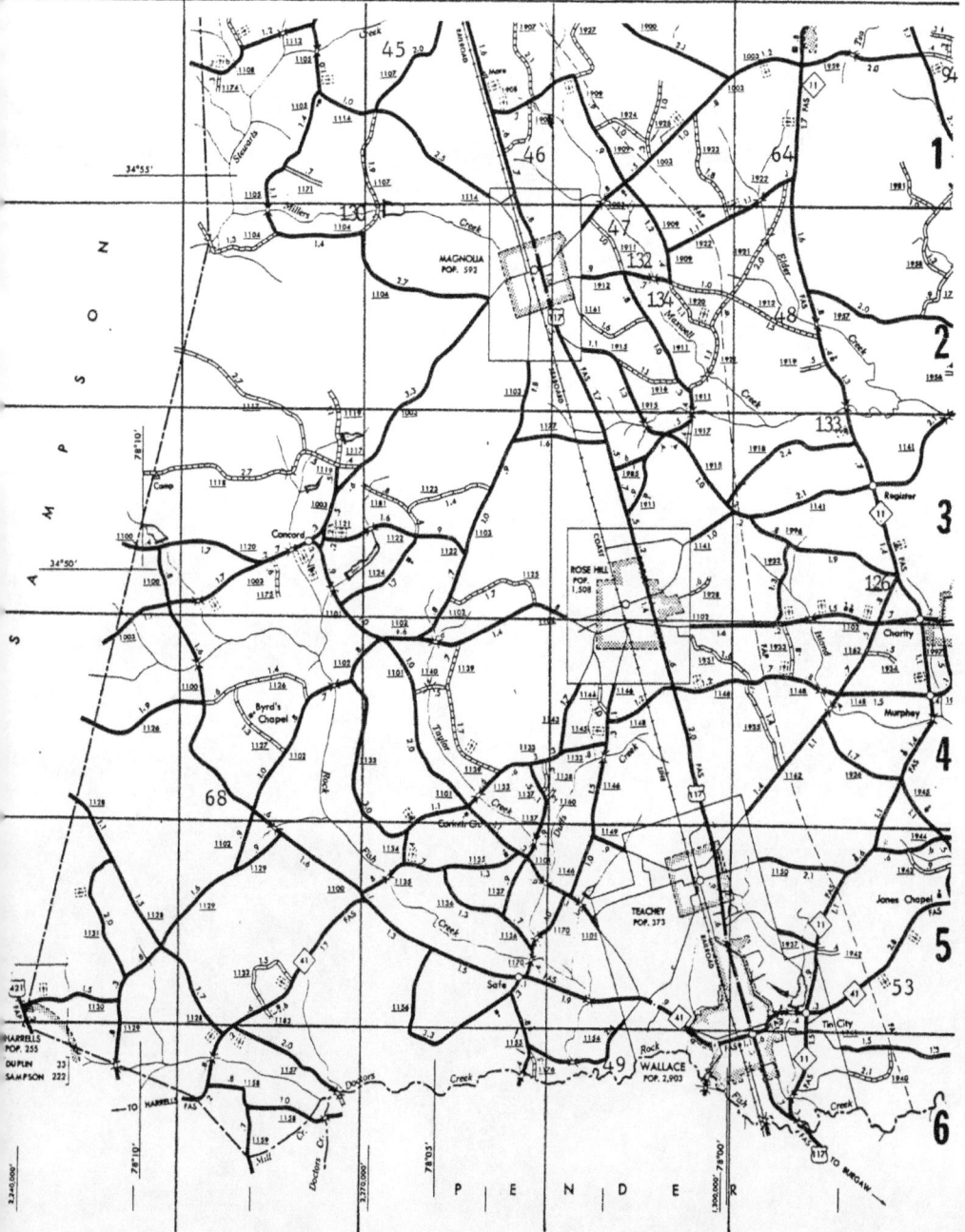

IV

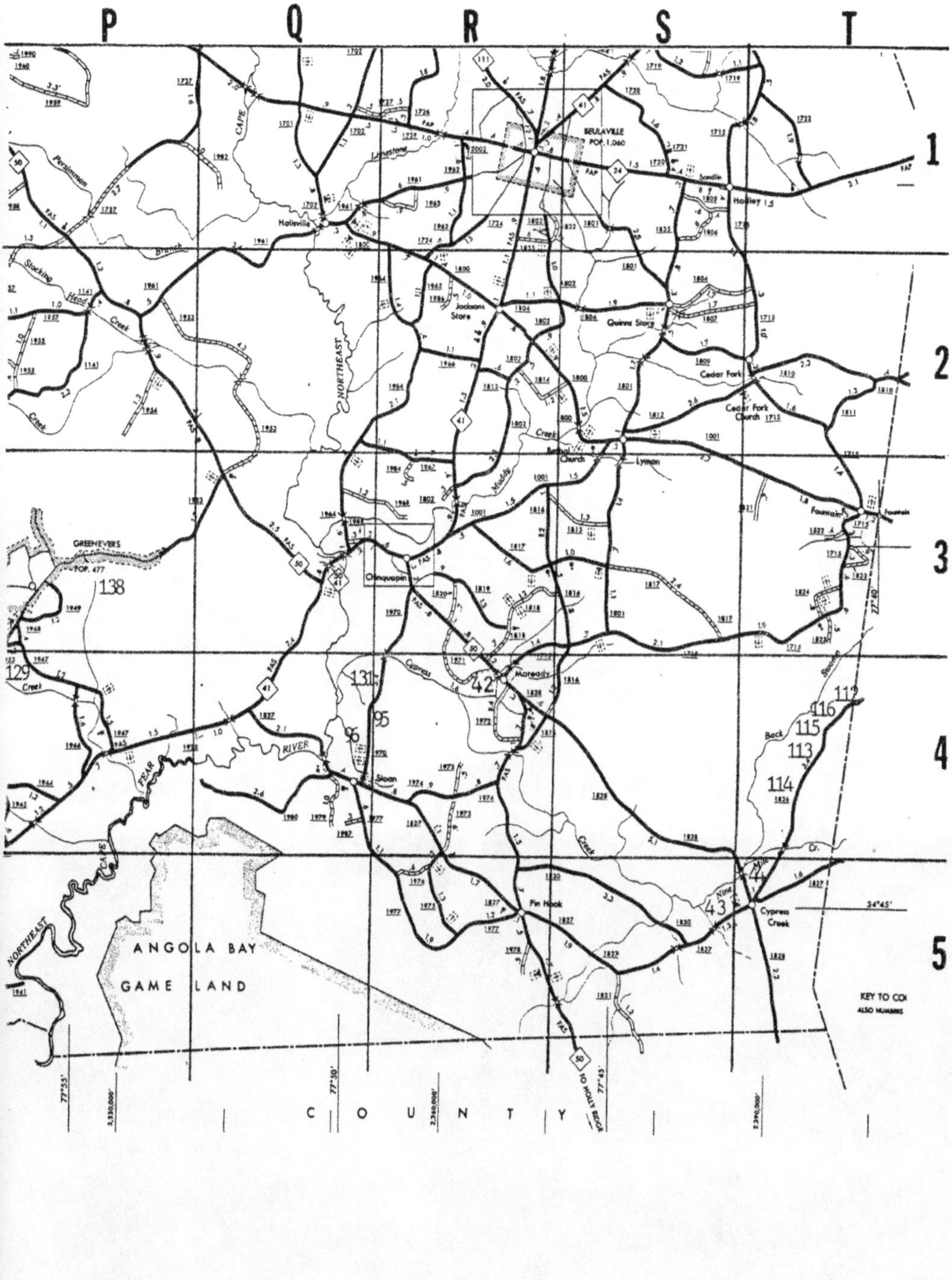
P
Q
R
S
T
1
2
3
4
5
BEULAVILLE
POP. 1,060
Hallsville
Limestone
Sandlin
Persimmon
Branch
Stocking
Head
Creek
Jacksons
Store
Quinns Store
Cedar Fork
Cedar Fork
Church
NORTHEAST
Muddy
Creek
Lyman
Fountain
GREENEVERS
POP. 477
Chinquapin
Maready
Cypress
Sloan
RIVER
FEAR
CAPE
Back
Pin Hook
Cypress
Creek
Nine
Mile
Cr.
ANGOLA BAY
GAME LAND
NORTHEAST
34°45'
77°40'
77°45'
77°50'
77°55'
KEY TO CO
ALSO NUMBERS
TO HOLLY RIDGE
C O U N T Y

CEMETERY INDEX

Page

ALPHIN H-2(74). 47

BEASLEY L-2(130). 78
BELL E-3(88). 53
BENNETT A-1(83) 52
BENNETT A-3(106). 62
BENNETT F-2(11) 9
BETHANY CHURCH H-3(102) 60
BLACKMORE A-4(50) 36
BLANCHARD A-6(117). 72
BLANCHARD R-4(95) 58
BLANTON N-6(49) 36
BLOUNT-LOFTIN B-4(122). 74
BOWDEN A-4(87). 53
BOWDEN-BROADHURST B-1(20) . . .15
BOYETTE A-5(67) 45
BRANCH ? (128). 78
BRICE O-5(53) 39
BRINSON O-1(94) 57
BROCK C-2(17) 13
BROCK D-2(59) 42
BROCK D-3(30) 22
BROWN-HORNE T-4(114). 70

CARR P-3(138) 81
CARROLL O-3(133). 79
CARTER B-4(99). 59
CARTER C-2(60). 43
CHERRY D-2(100) 59

DAIL E-3(89). 54
DAIL F-3(1) 1
DICKSON B-2(19) 14

FAISON C-3(104) 62
FAISON MEMORIAL A-2(65) 44

GARNER E-3(90). 54
GARNER F-2(127) 77
GARNER F-2(136) 80
GARNER F-2(56). 42
GRADY F-2(3). 4
GRADY H-3(51) 37
GRADY H-4(70) 45
GRADY MEMORIAL H-3(125) 76
GRADY MEMORIAL H-4(97). 58
GRANT C-3(105). 62
GUY I-3(78) 50

HALL Q-4(131) 78
HALSO-BATTS R-4(42) 31
HARDY C-3(108). 62

Page

HARDY H-1(110). 66
HERRING A-6(118). 72
HERRING F-2(12) 10
HERRING F-4(66) 44
HERRING G-3(111). 67
HERRING G-3(7). 6
HERRING H-1(71) 45
HODGES B-3(22). 16
HOLLINGSWORTH M-1(46) 34
HOLLOMAN B-1(85). 53
HOLMES F-2(58). 42
HOLMES F-3(2) 2
HOOKS C-3(107). 62
HORNE T-4(113). 68
HURST C-4(120). 73

JAMES S-5(43) 33
JONES D-1(33) 25
JONES G-3(13) 11
JONES H-2(72) 46
JONES-HARPER I-2(103) 61

KORNEGAY G-3(69). 45
KORNEGAY G-3(8) 7
KORNEGAY G-3(9) 7
KORNEGAY G-3(98). 59

LONG RIDGE CHURCH F-3(5). . . 5

MALLARD P-4(129). 78
MALPASS I-3(77) 49
MANNING T-4(115). 70
McARTHUR C-2(62). 43
McGOWEN E-5(6). 6
McGOWEN F-4(92) 57
MIDDLETON D-6(135). 80
MILLER C-3(23). 16
MOBLEY-MANNING T-4(116) . . .71
MORTON D-5(101) 60

NUNN G-1(37). 28

OUTLAW D-2(28). 21
OUTLAW D-3(27). 21
OUTLAW G-2(34). 25
OUTLAW G-2(35). 25
OUTLAW G-2(39). 28
OUTLAW MEMORIAL G-2(38) . . .28

PARKER D-3(26). 21
PEARSELL D-1(31). 24
PHILLIPS H-2(73). 46

Page

PHIPPS C-6(139). 81
PICKETT Q-4(96). 58
PRICE F-2(57). 42
PRIDGEN C-2(63). 43

RACKLEY O-2(48). 35
RAYNOR T-5(44) 34
REGISTER A-4(86) 53
RHODES B-3(21) 16
RITTER O-3(126). 77
ROBERTS D-3(16). 12
ROOTY BRANCH CHURCH E-3(109) . 63
ROUSE N-2(132) 79

SIMMONS G-2(41). 31
SOUTHERLAND C-3(79). 51
STANFORD MEMORIAL O-1(64). . . 44
STROUD H-2(40) 29
STROUD I-2(76) 47
SULLIVAN E-2(4). 4
SUMMERLIN E-3(25). 18
SUTTON A-1(84) 52
SUTTON B-2(52) 37
SWINSON C-2(61). 43
SWINSON C-3(24). 17
SWINSON-ROGERS N-2(132). . . . 79

TAYLOR A-1(80) 51
TAYLOR A-1(82) 51
TAYLOR F-2(10) 8
THOMAS N-2(47) 35
TILLMAN G-2(137) 80
TORRANS M-1(45). 34

UNDERHILL C-1(18). 14

WEEKS A-4(123) 75
WELLS-CARR N-2(134). 79
WHITFIELD D-1(32). 24
WHITFIELD F-2(55). 41
WHITFIELD G-2(36). 27
WHITFIELD G-2(75). 47
WHITMAN F-3(54). 41
WHITMAN G-4(14). 12
WHITMAN G-4(15). 12
WILKINS E-3(91). 56
WILLIAMS A-6(119). 73
WILLIAMS B-3(124). 75
WILLIAMS L-4(68) 45
WILLIAMS T-4(112). 67
WILLIAMS D-5(140). 81
WILLIAMSON F-4(93) 57
WINDERS D-2(29). 22
WRIGHT A-1(81) 51
WRIGHT-LOFTIN B-4(121) 74

A

ALEXANDER, James K. 20
ALEXANDER, Rovenia P. 20
ALFORD, Ruth Williams 73
ALPHIN, Ancie Taylor...........11
ALPHIN, Coreen Hill, Mrs. 9
ALPHIN, David.................47
ALPHIN, F.V. 19
ALPHIN, Florence..............19
ALPHIN, B.E. 19
ALPHIN, Garland O. 11
ALPHIN, Infant dau. 19
ALPHIN, J.D., Mr. & Mrs. 11
ALPHIN, John Tarnce...........11
ALPHIN, Katie Lucile..........11
ALPHIN, Mary E. 11
ALPHIN, Rebecca...............11
ALPHIN, Robert................11
ALPHIN, Tarnce................11
ALPHIN, Victoria..............11
ALPHIN, Victoria Turner.......11
ALPHIN, Yancey................11
ANDERSON, Sam 62
ANDERSON, Susan 62
ARNETTE, J. Franklin...........4

B

BAILEY, Henry K. 17
BAILEY, J.F. 17
BAILEY, M.F. 17
BARBREY, Allen................38
BARBREY, Betsey...............38
BARBREY, Cecil Allen..........38
BARBREY, Hettie...............38
BARBREY, Sarah Elva...........38
BARBREY, Thad. 38
BARBREY, Thaddeus Whitney.....38
BARNES, Eliza L. Cherry.......15
BARNES, L.F. 15
BARNES, L.T. 15
BARNETT, Burk H. 24
BARNETT, Stella Wood..........24
BARWICK, Infant................9
BARWICK, Mary L...............9
BARWICK, William R............9
BASS, Hettie F. 35
BASS, Julia Jones.............35
BASS, Mary J. 35
BASS, Mary Julia..............35
BASS, W.H. 35
BASS, William H. 35

BATCHELOR, Alf................67
BATCHELOR, Clender............31
BATCHELOR, Henry Mose 67
BATCHELOR, Infant son.........67
BATCHELOR, J.C. 67
BATCHELOR, J. Calvin 67
BATCHELOR, John S. 72
BATCHELOR, Lillie Belle.......31
BATCHELOR, Mary 72
BATCHELOR, Rosa...............67
BATCHELOR, Rosie B. 67
BATCHELOR, S.E. 67
BATCHELOR, Sallie.............67
BATCHELOR, Sarah..............67
BATCHELOR, Walter T. 67
BATTS, Arron.................68
BATTS, Beulah................31
BATTS, Burl S. 32
BATTS, Dora E. 32
BATTS, Isabel................71
BATTS, Jesse.................32
BATTS, John..................68
BATTS, John D................32
BATTS, John Ivey.............32
BATTS, L.J. 39
BATTS, Lois B. 31
BATTS, Lula..................32
BATTS, Margaret E. Brice.....39
BATTS, Martha................31
BATTS, Mary Elizabeth.....31,32
BATTS, Rachel L. 31
BATTS, Rudy..................31
BATTS, Simon.................70
BATTS, W.F. 31
BATTS, W.H. 31
BATTS, Zeb Thomas............71
BEASLEY, E. M. 78
BEASLEY, Lonnie D. 78
BEASLEY, Mattie C. [Corbett] ...78
BELL, baby boy...............24
BELL, Carrie Bennett.........54
BELL, Elias..................54
BELL, Elmore E. 54
BELL, Isadora................66
BELL, Johnnie Wilbert........54
BELL, Latha Jones............54
Bell, Lew A. 66
BELL, Mary Beth..............24
BELL, Math 54
BELL, Maude D. 53
BELL, Nathan H...............53
BELL, Peggy Sue..............54
BELL, Retha M. Jones.........54
BELL, Rosa B. 54
BELL, Rossie.................54

BELL, Scott..................54
BELL, Scott W. 54
BENNETT, Albert..............10
BENNETT, Albert S. 10
BENNETT, Benjamin Frank.......9
BENNETT, Bertha J. Waters....10
BENNETT, Currie D............10
BENNETT, Daniel R.............9
BENNETT, Easter Emmalina 62
BENNETT, Eula................10
BENNETT, Georgia Grace.......52
BENNETT, Harold F. 10
BENNETT, J.F. 52
BENNETT, James B. 55
BENNETT, Jimmy D..............9
BENNETT, John................55
BENNETT, John A. 62
BENNETT, John Anna............9
BENNETT, John H..............55
BENNETT, Laura H..............9
BENNETT, M.R. 52
BENNETT, Mary Barfield.......52
BENNETT, Mary Estelle........52
BENNETT, Mollie..............55
BENNETT, Nancy...............25
BENNETT, O.I. 52
BENNETT, S.L. 52
BENNETT, Tom.................25
BENNETT, V.E. 52
BEQUIS, Ethel K. 31
BISHOP, Ellen Dail............2
BISHOP, James Henry...........2
BIZZELL, Bessie E. 45
BIZZELL, J.B. 45
BIZZELL, John B. 45
BIZZELL, Laura E. 45
BLACKMON, Katie Peare........24
BLACKMON, Mabel Frances......24
BLACKMORE, Buckner L. 36
BLACKMORE, Emmett B. 36
BLACKMORE, Fedorah O.O. 37
BLACKMORE, Harold............36
BLACKMORE, Harold E. 36
BLACKMORE, Howard Edward......36
BLACKMORE, I.F. 37
BLACKMORE, Infant son........37
BLACKMORE, Janey Sansbury....36
BLACKMORE, Janie Belle.......37
BLACKMORE, Janie S. 37
BLACKMORE, Julia S. 36
BLACKMORE, Julia Sarepta.....36
BLACKMORE, Mary A. 37
BLACKMORE, Mary Aliff........36
BLACKMORE, Mary J. 36
BLACKMORE, Richard E. 37

BLACKMORE, Romulus W. 36
BLACKMORE, Wentworth F. 37
BLACKMORE, Willie..............37
BLACKMORE, Willie R. 36
BLAKE, Dicey A. 72
BLALOCK, George 63
BLALOCK, Sallie J. Taylor 63
BLANCHARD, Abram Washington 72
BLANCHARD, Bettie 58
BLANCHARD, Betty 58
BLANCHARD, Doris S. 58
BLANCHARD, John L. 72
BLANCHARD, Mattie Gaylor 58
BLANCHARD, Maury R. 58
BLANCHARD, Nancy Drew 72
BLANCHARD, Norwood Pitt 58
BLANCHARD, Wyatt Zachariah 58
BLANCHARD, Zachariah 58
BLANTON, C.R......................6
BLANTON, Maggie Emma............6
BLANTON, Mary.................36
BLANTON, Phebty Carolin.........36
BLANTON, T.B......................6
BLOUNT, J.W., Dr. 75
BLOUNT, Julia A. 74
BLOUNT, Maria G. Davis 75
BLOUNT, Samuel P. 74
BOWDEN, Annie.................15
BOWDEN, B.C. 53
BOWDEN, B.N. 14
BOWDEN, Benjamin..............53
BOWDEN, Benjamin Christopher....53
BOWDEN, Daniel................53
BOWDEN, Edney.................53
BOWDEN, Edney A. 53
BOWDEN, Ernest C. 15
BOWDEN, H.E. 53
BOWDEN, Heppie E. Jerman.......53
BOWDEN, John F. 53
BOWDEN, Levia B. 14
BOWDEN, Mary Louise............53
BOWDEN, Morehead..............53
BOWDEN, Penina................15
BOWDEN, Penina Cameron.........15
BOWDEN, S. 14
BOWDEN, S.A. 15
BOWDEN, S.E. 14
BOWDEN, Samuel Allen...........15
BOWDEN, W.S. 15
BOWDEN, William Henry..........14
BOYETTE, William..............45
BRADSHAW, Cecil...............39
BRADSHAW, O'Neal "Billy".......49
BRANCH, Archelous vii,78

BRANCH, Esther vii,78
BRICE, F.R. 40
BRICE, Francis................39
BRICE, George Vance............39
BRICE, John J. 39
BRICE, Margaret...............39
BRICE, Mary Florence...........40
BRICE, Mary Susan Bryant........39
BRICE, Nancy Watson............39
BRICE, O.W. 40
BRICE, Sarah W. 39
BRICE, William Dewey...........39
BRINSON, A. G. 57
BRINSON, A. J. 57
BRINSON, Amos J. 57
BRINSON, Annie Irene 57
BRINSON, Ashley G. 57
BRINSON, Cora 57
BRINSON, Cora Bostic 57
BRINSON, Eleanor Louise 57
BRINSON, Emma 57
BRINSON, Eva 57
BRINSON, F. A. 57
BRINSON, Florence A. 57
BRINSON, H. J. 57
BRINSON, Hiram J. 57
BRINSON, Infant dau. 57
BRINSON, Infant son 57
BRINSON, Irene 57
BRINSON, J. B. 57
BRINSON, Jesse B. 57
BRINSON, L. H. 57
BRINSON, Leroy H. 57
BRINSON, Mary E. 57
BRITT, Infant son.............30
BRITT, Jean Garner............29
BRITT, Lester.................30
BRITT, Lester Lee, Jr. 29
BRITT, Lester Lee, Sr. 29
BRITT, Margaret...............30
BRITT, Margaret Stroud.........29
BROADHURST, Allen Manley........15
BROADHURST, Clyde Lewis.........15
BROADHURST, Helen C. 15
BROADHURST, John..............15
BROADHURST, John Allen.........15
BROCK, Elizabeth J. 24
BROCK, Francenia..............23
BROCK, George W. 24
BROCK, Henry..................13
BROCK, Henry Herman...........13
BROCK, Hollon.................24
BROCK, Infant son.............13
BROCK, Jesse H................42

BROCK, Leslie Ray..............23
BROCK, Lucinda................42
BROCK, Mack...................23
BROCK, Mallie.................13
BROCK, Minnie Lee.............23
BROCK, Randal.................43
BROCK, Sallie Leona...........13
BROGDEN, D.B..................38
BROGDEN, Laurence S. 38
BROGDEN, M.E..................38
BROGDEN, Mary Etta............38
BROOKS, Flora Alice Beasley 78
BROOKS, George 78
BROOKS, Infant dau. 78
BROWING?, Wellie W. 52
BROWN, Annie C. 33
BROWN, Clyde..................70
BROWN, Cyrus J. 70
BROWN, Estella B. 36
BROWN, Ethel W. 31
BROWN, Harold Kenneth..........36
BROWN, Infant son.............34
BROWN, Ira....................36
BROWN, J.W....................70
BROWN, Jacob..................70
BROWN, Johnny T...............79
BROWN, L.D....................33
BROWN, Larry E................69
BROWN, Linnie H...............70
BROWN, Mary E.................70
BROWN, Mary Eliza.............70
BROWN, Mattie B. Horne.........69
BROWN, Mora Estelle Carr.......79
BROWN, Robert L...............31
BROWN, S.A. 31
BROWN, S.D. 33
BROWN, Sarah E. Williams.......68
BROWN, Seba...................70
BROWN, Stephen................70
BROWN, Teresa Michelle.........70
BROWN, Thelbert Morris.........70
BROWN, W.W. 68
BROWN, Winford L. 70
BROWNING, Connie..............52
BROWNING, Connie Eva Bennett....52
BROWNING, Granger G. 52
BROWNING, Infant dau. 52
BROWNING, R.J.................52
BROWNING, Robert James........52
BUCHAN, Earl...................9
BUCHAN, J.J. 9
BUCHAN, Joseph J. 9
BUCHAN, Lillie..................9

C

CARR, Amanda E. 81
CARR, G.S. (cemetery)..........79
CARR, Infant son...............81
CARR, J.D. 81
CARR, J.O. 81
CARR, Jacob David..............81
CARR, James Owen 81
CARR, James...............vii,81
CARR, Jas. O. 81
CARR, M.A. 81
CARR, Mary Ann Wells...........81
CARR, Mary W. 81
CARR, Nancy 81
CARR, Sarah Catharine..........81
CARR, Walter R. 81
CARROLL, Ann vii,79
CARROLL, John.............vii,79
CARTER, A.H. 43
CARTER, Alma B.................4
CARTER, Archie W. 40
CARTER, Ashford................43
CARTER, Atlas Harvey...........43
CARTER, Beatrice...............43
CARTER, Beatrice Williamson....43
CARTER, Calvin Lowell..........43
CARTER, Charlie Herbert 59
CARTER, Daisy C. 39
CARTER, Doris H. 40
CARTER, Edd G..................4
CARTER, Eddie L. 50
CARTER, Emma H. 40
CARTER, Fannie M...............4
CARTER, Geo. 50
CARTER, George.................50
CARTER, Henry. 40
CARTER, Infant son.............43
CARTER, Joseph L. 39
CARTER, L.H. 50
CARTER, Louise Holmes..........43
CARTER, Mary E. 40
CARTER, Molly..................40
CARTER, Myrtie.................50
CARTER, O.W. 40
CARTER, Octavia, Mrs. 43
CARTER, Oscar S. 39
CARTER, Rayford H. 40
CARTER, Raymond................50
CARTER, Sarah E. 40
CARTER, T.H., Rev. 40
CARTER, Thomas H., Jr. 40
CARTER, Viola T. 39

CARTER, William Alsie 59
CARTER, Willie.................40
CARTER, Willie T. 40
CARTER, Winnie Dell............40
CAVENAUGH, Infant son..........33
CAVENAUGH, M.E. 33
CAVENAUGH, O.D. 33
CAVENAUGH, R.F. 33
CAVENAUGH, R.M. 33
CHERRY, Andrew Franklin 60
CHERRY, Bryant W. 15
CHERRY, Callie.................60
CHERRY, Dorothy May 60
CHERRY, Elbert Romy 60
CHERRY, Ellen 60
CHERRY, Finnie Talamage 59
CHERRY, G. W. 60
CHERRY, George Washington 60
CHERRY, Gertrude...............20
CHERRY, Jim 60
CHERRY, Julia A. 15
CHERRY, Lee C. 15
CHERRY, Lemuel 60
CHERRY, Lottie Ruth 60
CHERRY, Margaret Ann 60
CHERRY, Mary J. 60
CHERRY, Mattie Ruth 60
CHERRY, Ruth 60
CHERRY, Ruth Meeks 60
CHERRY, Samuel C. 20
CHERRY, William D. 60
CHERRY, Willie 60
CHERRY, Willis D. 60
CHESTNUTT, D. J. 64
CHESTNUTT, Daniel James 64
CHESTNUTT, Eunice 64
CHESTNUTT, Harriett 64
CHESTNUTT, Henry Preston 64
CHESTNUTT, Herritte 64
CHESTNUTT, Lissie Bell 64
CHESTNUTT, Scott 64
CLINTON, Richard...............51
COLEY, Elisha J. 53
COLLINS, James [M.?] 74
COLLINS, Mary Jane 74

D

DAIL, Ann......................2
DAIL, Ann Wiley................1
DAIL, Baby 56
DAIL, Budd.....................1
DAIL, Cassie 56

DAIL, Claude...................54
DAIL, Coris Gerald.............1
DAIL, Daisy....................55
DAIL, Delia A..................2
DAIL, Della....................2
DAIL, Della E..................2
DAIL, Della Frances Kornegay...2
DAIL, Della K..................2
DAIL, Dobson...................56
DAIL, Doris Robinson...........2
DAIL, Edward A. 56
DAIL, Ellen....................2
DAIL, Erastus..................55
DAIL, Eugene...................2
DAIL, Faison...................2
DAIL, Florie Ann...............56
DAIL, Forrest..................54
DAIL, Glennie 55
DAIL, Grace....................1
DAIL, Griza....................1
DAIL, Grizza D.................1
DAIL, Haywood Baines...........55
DAIL, Henry Oliver.............2
DAIL, Herbert..................10
DAIL, Howell...................1
DAIL, Infant...................1
DAIL, Infant son...............1
DAIL, Iris Carol...............1
DAIL, John Donald..............2
DAIL, Jonah....................2
DAIL, Jonas....................1
DAIL, Lawrence Albert..........2
DAIL, Leacy Jones..............1
DAIL, Lela Swinson.............54
DAIL, Loney B. 54
DAIL, Lula M. 56
DAIL, Mallie Taylor............2
DAIL, Marable..................1
DAIL, Marvin...................1
DAIL, Mary Francis.............2
DAIL, Mary Ruth................56
DAIL, Mary Whitman.............2
DAIL, Mathie Buck..............2
DAIL, Robert Jackson...........1
DAIL, Rosa D...................2
DAIL, Sallie...................1
DAIL, Sampson..................2
DAIL, Sarah Jane...............1
DAIL, Sonnie J.................1
DAIL, Tallins..................2
DAIL, Walter M. 55
DAIL, Wilson...................2
DAIL, Winlson..................1
DAILY, George..................7

98

DAILY, Mary E. 7
DAVENPORT, L.J. 46
DAVENPORT, Maggie O. 46
DAVIS, Calvin..................3
DAVIS, Daisey..................3
DAVIS, Daisy Singleton.........3
DAVIS, Jim.....................2
DAVIS, Kattie Belle............3
DAVIS, Milfred Ray.............3
DAVIS, Mittie..................3
DAVIS, Ruth G. 51
DAVIS, Ruth Jean..............51
DAVIS, W.H. 51
DEMPSEY, Ann L. 39
DEMPSEY, G.F. 39
DICKSON, Ann Clopton..........14
DICKSON, Anne Eliza...........14
DICKSON, James G., Dr. 14
DICKSON, Joseph L. 14
DICKSON, Sallie J. 14
DICKSON, Sallie Jane..........14
DIXON, _?_....................14
DIXON, James W. 15
DIXON, Jim W. 15
DIXON, Mary J. 15
DIXON, Wellie E. 15
DUNCAN, Bobby.................80
DUNCAN, Thelma................80
DUNCAN, Thelma Tillman........80
DUNCAN, Thelma Tillman Mrs. ..81
DUPREE, William D. 29

E

EATMON, Esther B. 24
EATMON, George O. 24
EATMON, Raymond A. 24
EATMON, Robert E. 24
EATMON, Robert E. Jr. 24
EZZELL, Clarice 63
EZZELL, Clarice E. 63
EZZELL, Infant son 63
EZZELL, Joshua.................37
EZZELL, Joshua R. 73
EZZELL, Nancy 73
EZZELL, Patrick vii,73
EZZELL, Ransom 63

F

FAGG, Daniel 77
FAISON, Diana Griffin......vii,44
FAISON, Elizabeth 62
FAISON, Henry..............vii,44

FAISON, Lilias Serena 62
FAISON, William W. 62
FARRIOR, Susan 78
FONVIELLE, E. W. 73
FONVIELLE, Infant son 73
FONVIELLE, N. S. 73
FORD, B.D. 37
FORD, S.E. 37
FUTRELL, Bettie Batts..........32
FUTRELL, George N. 32

G

GARNER, Alice Udorah...........42
GARNER, Annie Bell.............42
GARNER, Annie S. 55
GARNER, Annie W. 42
GARNER, Annie Whitfield........42
GARNER, Cora Bessie 55
GARNER, Dora Bessie............55
GARNER, F.D. 80
GARNER, Florence Isedore Dail..80
GARNER, Furnander Price........42
GARNER, Henry 77
GARNER, Isaac Webster 55
GARNER, J.J. 42
GARNER, J.J., Jr. 42
GARNER, James C. 80
GARNER, Jeff 55
GARNER, Joel J. 42
GARNER, Joseph J. 42
GARNER, Lottie H. 55
GARNER, Marion Franklin 55
GARNER, Morris "Wheeler" 55
GARNER, Moses Daniel 55
GARNER, Nathan 77
GARNER, Penelope Kornegay 77
GARNER, S. 55,80
GARNER, Sarah 55
GARNER, Simeon.............55,80
GARNER, V.R. Mrs. 77,80
GARNER, Vina Dail 55
GARNER, Zeb....................55
GARNER, Zeb V. 55
GARRIS, Estelle Jones..........41
GARRIS, T.W. 41
GHLIGHEN, Edward...............22
GHLIGHEN, Infant son...........22
GHLIGHEN, Martha...............22
GLISSON, Haywood 59
GLISSON, Susan Linda 59
GOODMAN, Ann Eliza 65
GOODMAN, Annie G. 11
GOODMAN, Christine 64

GOODMAN, David.................11
GOODMAN, Foye 64
GOODMAN, Foye Jr. 64
GOODMAN, George Robert 65
GOODMAN, Infant 64
GOODMAN, Infant son 64
GOODMAN, Mable Outlaw 64
GOODMAN, Nettie 64
GOODMAN, Nettie Brown 64
GORDON, Flossie B. 52
GORDON, M.....................35
GORDON, Richard...............35
GORDON, Susie.................35
GOUGH, Robert W. 25
GRADY, A. O. 77
GRADY, Alexander 58,76
GRADY, Alexander Outlaw 76
GRADY, Anne 58
GRADY, B. W. 77
GRADY, Bryan Whitfield 76
GRADY, Byron..................37
GRADY, Celie..................37
GRADY, Charity 58
GRADY, Clarissa 76
GRADY, Edith B. 29
GRADY, Eliza Catherine........37
GRADY, Elizabeth 58
GRADY, Elizabeth Outlaw ...vii,76
GRADY, Ella S. 28
GRADY, Ethel M. 37
GRADY, Frederick 29,58
GRADY, Gibson 77
GRADY, Glennie W...............4
GRADY, H. P. 76
GRADY, Henry G. 45
GRADY, Henry vii,76
GRADY, Infant sons............28
GRADY, Ira Albert..............4
GRADY, J.C. 28
GRADY, J. McR. 37
GRADY, James E., Sr. 19
GRADY, James Earl, Sr. 19
GRADY, John Jr. 58
GRADY, John vii,37,58,76
GRADY, Julia A. 77
GRADY, K.V. 37
GRADY, Katie V. 37
GRADY, Lewis 58
GRADY, Lucille W. 12
GRADY, Margaret 58
GRADY, Mary 37,58
GRADY, Mary Whitfield 58,76
GRADY, Mildred Kelly Summerlin..19
GRADY, Nancy (Sloan) 76

GRADY, Nancy W. 77
GRADY, O. A. 77
GRADY, Patrick H. 76
GRADY, Rachel Elizabeth 77
GRADY, Repsy 76
GRADY, Robert J. 37
GRADY, W.J. 37
GRADY, William 58
GRADY, William J. 37
GRANT, Belle 62
GRANT, Margaret C. 62
GRANT, Margaret C. Dobson 62
GRANT, Oscar C. 62
GRANT, Stafford 62
GREEN, Loys 65
GUY, Infant son 46
GUY, J.O. 46,50
GUY, John Owen...................51
GUY, Marion Nixon...............50
GUY, S.O. 46,50
GUY, Sadie Oda..................51

H

HALL, A. J. 78
HALL, Asha Chestnut 78
HALL, Ella Thomas 78
HALL, Infant dau. 78
HALL, Martha Helen 78
HALL, S. E. 78
HALL, Stephen Edward 78
HALSO, Ada Charlotte............33
HALSO, E.A. 32
HALSO, Eliza Elizabeth..........33
HALSO, Estella R. 33
HALSO, J.D., Mr. & Mrs. 33
HALSO, J.G. 32
HALSO, J.W., Mr. & Mrs. 33
HALSO, James H. 32
HALSO, John.....................33
HALSO, John Dewey..............33
HALSO, John W. 33
HALSO, Kattie Alma.............33
HALSO, Lou Ella.................33
HALSO, Marie....................33
HALSO, Norman...................33
HALSO, Palmetto.................33
HALSO, Reynold..................33
HARDY, A. J. 63
HARDY, Alonzo 66
HARDY, Alonzo, Jr. 66
HARDY, Andrew J. 63
HARDY, Catharine 63
HARDY, Charity 63

HARDY, Egbert 63
HARDY, Elender 66
HARDY, Ellen 66
HARDY, Herman 66
HARDY, Ira T. 63
HARDY, Jesse 66
HARDY, John H. 63
HARDY, Phineas 63
HARDY, Sarah Worley 66
HARPER, Alcy A. 75
HARPER, Arlene Lee 62
HARPER, Betty S. 62
HARPER, Daniel 75
HARPER, Daniel D. 75
HARPER, Felix 62
HARPER, Herbert Allen 62
HARPER, James A. 61
HARPER, James Allen 61
HARPER, Julia Ann 61
HARPER, Lola 62
HARPER, Lola Thompson 62
HARPER, Luba 62
HARPER, Luby 62
HARPER, Luby, Jr. 62
HARPER, P. J. 75
HARPER, Sammie 62
HARPER, Tesia C. 62
HATCH, Eliza Jane Hooks.....vii,62
HATCH, Infant 62
HATCHER, Annie Mariah...........37
HEATH, Susan E. Blanton........36
HEATH, W.A. 36
HENDERSON, Burras W. 69
HERRING, Abba E. 67
HERRING, Ada Grady 60
HERRING, Annie E. 66
HERRING, B.F. 67
HERRING, Ben.....................67
HERRING, Benjamin F. 67
HERRING, Bertha..................67
HERRING, Carrie Inez.............6
HERRING, Cena Harper 61
HERRING, Charity E. 10
HERRING, Charlie................50
HERRING, Clifton H..............7
HERRING, Connie S................7
HERRING, Cuzzie Jane............45
HERRING, Daniel...............7,44
HERRING, Daniel Jr................6
HERRING, Daniel R................6
HERRING, Delia..................10
HERRING, Delia Catherine.......49
HERRING, Della...............7,50
HERRING, Delphia E..............7

HERRING, Elisha.............vii,39
HERRING, Ella J. 66
HERRING, Emma....................15
HERRING, Eula Mae 60
HERRING, Fannie..................10
HERRING, Fred....................7
HERRING, George Glanton.........10
HERRING, Gid.....................10
HERRING, Henry....................6
HERRING, Henry E..................6
HERRING, I. W. 72
HERRING, Inez.....................6
HERRING, Infant..................10
HERRING, Jeff.....................7
HERRING, John L. 15
HERRING, John R. 49
HERRING, John William...........45
HERRING, Johnie Randal...........6
HERRING, Johnnie M.A. 15
HERRING, Julia...................10
HERRING, Kathleen Carter 59
HERRING, Katie C. 72
HERRING, Laney...................10
HERRING, Lannie..................10
HERRING, Lizzie 10,67
HERRING, Marian Hardy...........10
HERRING, Mary....................39
HERRING, Nancy W..................3
HERRING, Needham.................10
HERRING, Park....................10
HERRING, Patience................46
HERRING, Pearl P..................7
HERRING, R. V. 72
HERRING, Rachel.............vii,44
HERRING, Samuel U. 60
HERRING, Simpson.................10
HERRING, Stephen A. 46
HERRING, Thurman.................50
HERRING, Virginia.................7
HERRING, William M................1
HERRING, Winnie...................6
HERRING, Winnie E.................6
HILL, Cleveland..................49
HILL, Mary J. 49
HILL, Randy D. 61
HILL, Ronald Lane...............49
HINSON, Hazel Summerlin.........19
HINSON, Randolph.................41
HINSON, Walter Lee..............19
HOBBS, P.B. 52
HODGES, Holloway...........vii,16
HOLLAND, Benson 59
HOLLAND, Charlie................50
HOLLAND, Infant son 59

HOLLAND, John....................9
HOLLAND, Joseph..................51
HOLLAND, Lottie C. 59
HOLLAND, Nancy Jane.............52
HOLLAND, Wennieford.............50
HOLLAND, Winnie.................50
HOLLINGSWORTH, A. 35
HOLLINGSWORTH, Alfred...........35
HOLLINGSWORTH, E.A. 34
HOLLINGSWORTH, E.D. 35
HOLLINGSWORTH, Ezra Alice Johnson34
HOLLINGSWORTH, Fred O. 35
HOLLINGSWORTH, Infant son....34,35
HOLLINGSWORTH, John Owen........35
HOLLINGSWORTH, K.E. 34
HOLLINGSWORTH, Kilby...........34
HOLLINGSWORTH, Mary A. 35
HOLLINGSWORTH, Mary Eliser......34
HOLLINGSWORTH, Pearl...........35
HOLLINGSWORTH, S.J. 35
HOLLINGSWORTH, Sallie..........35
HOLLINGSWORTH, Sarah Jane.......35
HOLLINGSWORTH, Susan A. 35
HOLLINGSWORTH, Virginia Lenora..34
HOLLOMAN, Lizzie................53
HOLMES, Betty....................6
HOLMES, Beulah...................3
HOLMES, Callie Homes.............3
HOLMES, Clayton F................6
HOLMES, Gerutrude B. Garner.....42
HOLMES, Hadie Lou................3
HOLMES, Joel....................42
HOLMES, John.....................3
HOLMES, Leroy....................6
HOLMES, Major....................6
HOLMES, Mary.....................3
HOLMES, Mary Sue.................3
HOLMES, Susan....................5
HOLMES, Viola W..................6
HONEYCUTT, W.H. 47
HOOKS, Ann......................62
HOOKS, Charles 62
HORN, Benjamin A. 68
HORN, Howel.....................70
HORN, Mattie B. 69
HORNE, A.D. 69
HORNE, Alfred D. 68
HORNE, Alvania..................70
HORNE, Barbara..................69
HORNE, Berry....................69
HORNE, Clara....................70
HORNE, Cornelius................69
HORNE, Dennie W. 69
HORNE, Edward...................69

HORNE, Edwin 71
HORNE, Elouise..................69
HORNE, Emma H. 69
HORNE, H.N. 69
HORNE, Henry L. 70
HORNE, Holland J. 69
HORNE, Hosea E. 68
HORNE, Howard...................70
HORNE, Howell Thomas............70
HORNE, Infant...................69
HORNE, Isaac E. 69
HORNE, J. W. 71
HORNE, Jethro A. 67
HORNE, Johnnie N. 69
HORNE, K.T. 69
HORNE, L.T. 69
HORNE, Lindsey Right............69
HORNE, Lonnie...................70
HORNE, Luther H. 70
HORNE, Lydia B. 71
HORNE, Mammie B. 68
HORNE, Mannie...................69
HORNE, Mary S. 68
HORNE, Mattie C. Manning........71
HORNE, Olive....................69
HORNE, Perry S. 69
HORNE, Ralph 71
HORNE, Roy......................69
HORNE, Sealie C. 68
HORNE, Thaddus L. 69
HORNE, Viola A. 67
HORNE, Watson...................70
HORNE, William McKinley.........68
HOWARD, Annie B. 20
HOWARD, Bettie..................20
HOWARD, J.W. 20
HOWARD, John T. 65
HOWARD, Lula Mae C. 12
HOWELL, Mamie....................1
HURST, Margaret vii,74
HURST, Robert K. 73
HURST, William vii,74
HUSSEY, Elizabeth S. 30
HUSSEY, Kator B. 30

J

JACKSON, C. Henry...............41
JACKSON, Charlie Franklin.......41
JACKSON, Evangeline.............41
JACKSON, Gertrude M. 41
JACKSON, girls, two.............43
JACKSON, Harriet Grady 77
JACKSON, Martha 77

JACKSON, Norah..................41
JACKSON, Norah W. 41
JACKSON, W.J. 41
JACKSON, William Edward.........41
JAMES, Barbara..................34
JAMES, Beulah B. 68
JAMES, Christopher C. 17
JAMES, David....................34
JAMES, Elizabeth A. Batts.......33
JAMES, Isaac....................34
JAMES, John P. 17
JAMES, Lonie B. 33
JAMES, Mary S. Swinson..........17
JAMES, Obedience Joyner.........17
JAMES, Relmond D. 68
JAMES, Robert...................33
JENKINS, Bessie South 61
JENNETTE, Edna L. 38
JENNETTE, Floyd L. 38
JENNETTE, William H. 38
JERNIGAN, Allen.................19
JERNIGAN, Annie.................19
JERNIGAN, Annie D. Summerlin....19
JERNIGAN, Cornelia K. Summerlin.19
JERNIGAN, John Allen............19
JERNIGAN, Rosedene Sloan........19
JERNIGAN, T.A. 19
JERNIGAN, Thurman Allen.........19
JINNETTE, Henry Carl............38
JINNETTE, Leonard L. 38
JONES, Aga......................54
JONES, Aja......................54
JONES, Alonzo 64
JONES, Amos J. 46
JONES, Andrew 61
JONES, Andrew F. 61
JONES, Ashley...................11
JONES, Ashley E. Tew............41
JONES, Callie Grady.............11
JONES, Daniel Edward 65
JONES, Dora 64
JONES, Dora 64
JONES, Eldridge.................32
JONES, Elijah F. 25
JONES, Ella.....................25
JONES, Emma.....................25
JONES, Enos D. 64
JONES, Enous D. 65
JONES, F. A. 44,64
JONES, Festeus T. 25
JONES, Furney A. 64
JONES, Gilbert 64
JONES, Haddie 65
JONES, Hadie 64

JONES, Infant 61
JONES, James A. 61
JONES, Jennie................5
JONES, John Henry................5
JONES, Johnny T. 61
JONES, Julia 64
JONES, Julius R. 44
JONES, L. 25
JONES, Leonard H. 61
JONES, Lewis................5
JONES, Lewis H. 61
JONES, Lewis Nelson 61
JONES, Lillie C. 64
JONES, Lou Ellen H. 61
JONES, Louise C. 61
JONES, Ludia 61
JONES, Ludia W. 61
JONES, M. B. 25
JONES, Mabel W. 20
JONES, Major................41
JONES, Major W. 61
JONES, Martha E. 68
JONES, Mary................39
JONES, Mary F. 25
JONES, Mary Thigpen................1
JONES, Minnie Whaley................32
JONES, Mollie................44
JONES, N. Franklin 61
JONES, Oliver 64
JONES, Pearl H. 61
JONES, Phillip................1
JONES, R.W. 25
JONES, Rachel W. 25
JONES, Russell Dean 64
JONES, Sarah Dail................2
JONES, Sarah Kornegay................54
JONES, Sarah Winnifred 61
JONES, Susan A. 12
JONES, Thaddeus................25
JONES, W.N. 2
JONES, Walter................20
JONES, Willard A. 46
JONES, William H. 39
JONES, Zular 65
JOYNER, Alton................12
JOYNER, Calhoun H. 13
JOYNER, Sallie G. 13

K

KALMAR, John Nicholas 63
KALMAR, William Christopher 63
KELLY, Bertie O. Simmons................31
KELLY, W.H. (Tom)................31

KENNEDY, C.G. 23
KENNEDY, Charlie G. 23
KENNEDY, Essie................23
KENNEDY, Essie B. 23
KENNEDY, Gladys 73
KENNEDY, J.T. 73
KENNEDY, Lavinia 73
KETCHAM, E. Elane................31
KING, George................79
KING, Infants 79
KING, Maude................79
KOONCE, David Marion 74
KOONCE, Francis Loftin 74
KOONCE, Winfield E. 74
KORNEGAY, A.E. 7
KORNEGAY, Abram 59
KORNEGAY, Alice................7
KORNEGAY, Alice Daly................8
KORNEGAY, Annie................8
KORNEGAY, Annie E. 7
KORNEGAY, Arrie................7,8
KORNEGAY, Arthur................8
KORNEGAY, Beulah Summerlin................5
KORNEGAY, Bob 59
KORNEGAY, C.J. 59
KORNEGAY, Charles J. 59
KORNEGAY, Daniel................8
KORNEGAY, Daniel Lee................5
KORNEGAY, Daniel Richard................5
KORNEGAY, DeLeon 80
KORNEGAY, Duff................8
KORNEGAY, Elbert F. 5
KORNEGAY, Eliza Cornella................45
KORNEGAY, Elizabeth K. 8
KORNEGAY, Ernest J. 80
KORNEGAY, Evelyn W. 8
KORNEGAY, Fisher 59
KORNEGAY, George F. Sr. 59
KORNEGAY, George R. 8
KORNEGAY, H.B.,Sr. Mrs. 14,39
KORNEGAY, Harold 59
KORNEGAY, Harvey................7
KORNEGAY, Henry R. 59
KORNEGAY, Henry R., Rev. 59
KORNEGAY, Infant dau................7
KORNEGAY, Infant son................7
KORNEGAY, J.D. 7
KORNEGAY, J.F. 7
KORNEGAY, J. Fisher................7
KORNEGAY, Jennette 59
KORNEGAY, Joseph F. 7
KORNEGAY, Laura................7
KORNEGAY, Lola E. Smith................8
KORNEGAY, Louise................8

KORNEGAY, Lucy 59
KORNEGAY, Martha J. 8
KORNEGAY, Mary A. G. 59
KORNEGAY, Mary Green 59
KORNEGAY, Matthew J. 7
KORNEGAY, N.D. 7
KORNEGAY, Nick................7
KORNEGAY, Ollie................7
KORNEGAY, Rachel Jones................5
KORNEGAY, Randolph................8
KORNEGAY, Richard A. 5
KORNEGAY, Robert D. 45
KORNEGAY, Russell W. 80
KORNEGAY, Sallie M. 80
KORNEGAY, Sarah 59
KORNEGAY, Sarah A. 59
KORNEGAY, Swannie Belle................45
KORNEGAY, Thomas J. 8
KORNEGAY, W.R. 7
KORNEGAY, Wade H. 59
KORNEGAY, Wooten................7,8
KORNEGAY, Zilphia................7
KORNEGAY, Zilphia F. Smith................7

L

LAMB, Eula L. 18
LAMM, Willie Clifton................9
LANE, John Robert (infant)................80
LANE, Lola May Tillman................80
LANE, Raymond................80
LANGSTON, Charlie Jane................50
LANGSTON, I.D. 50
LANGSTON, Randolph................50
LANIER, B.J. 41
LANIER, Bonnie................41
LANIER, Elizabeth Parker................33
LANIER, Henrietta................33
LANIER, Jeremiah................33
LAWS, William Grady, Mrs. 58
LEE, Annie B. 49
LEE, Annie Sasser 75
LEE, Henry................49
LEE, Infant son & dau. 49
LOFTIN, Barbara................25
LOFTIN, Ellanora 75
LOFTIN, Emma A. 75
LOFTIN, Ernestine 75
LOFTIN, Fannie V. 75
LOFTIN, Franklin 74
LOFTIN, Joel................39
LOFTIN, L. R. 74
LOFTIN, Liston L. 75
LOFTIN, Little Martha 74

LOFTIN, Luther R. 74
LOFTIN, Oscar 74
LOFTIN, S. 74
LOFTIN, Susan 74
LOFTIN, Susan H. 74
LOFTIN, Susan H. 75
LOFTIN, V. C. 75
LOFTIN, Victoria C. Blount 75
LOFTIN, W. S. 75

M

MALLARD, Barbara vii,78
MALLARD, Dickson 78
MALLARD, John vii,78
MALLARD, Mary M. 78
MALPASS, Birtie T. 50
MALPASS, Carrie..................50
MALPASS, J.M. 50
MALPASS, Joel M. 50
MALPASS, Stella..................50
MALPASS, Stella May..............50
MALPASS, Thurman.................50
MALPASS, Wm. 50
MANNING, Albert 72
MANNING, Dunn 71
MANNING, Helen 71
MANNING, Hugh....................71
MANNING, Infant son 71
MANNING, John L. 71
MANNING, Johnnie D. ...68,70,71,72
MANNING, Many N. 71
MANNING, Marten..................71
MANNING, Merritt.................71
MANNING, Neal 71
MANNING, Piranda 71
MANNING, Sarah A. 71
MANNING, Serena Catherine.......71
MANNING, Susan J. 71
MANNING, Sutton..................71
MARSHBURN, Selma E. Herring 67
MARTIN, Loy Leonadas.............32
McARTHUR, Charlie................43
McARTHUR, Linwood E. 43
McARTHUR, Ora M. 43
McEACHERN, Leora H. 39,79
McGOWEN, Hannah Green vii,57
McGOWEN, James H. 6
McGOWEN, Joseph vii,57
McGOWEN, Margia S. Stokes........6
MERCER, Joe......................43
MERCER, Mary King................43
MERRITT, Bessie O.Q. 29
MEWBORN, Edith...................26

MEWBORN, Infant dau. 26
MEWBORN, Infant son.............26
MEWBORN, Moses T. 26
MIDDLETON, A.W. 80
MIDDLETON, B.F. 80
MIDDLETON, E.A. 80
MIDDLETON, Mary Delila..........80
MIDDLETON, W.B. 80
MIDDLETON, Wm. B. 80
MILLER, Annie E. 16
MILLER, Bethania J. 17
MILLER, Charlie William.........17
MILLER, Clara....................16
MILLER, Eliza Mae...............17
MILLER, Elizabeth T. 17
MILLER, George W. 23
MILLER, Hez L. 17
MILLER, J.R. 17
MILLER, James William...........17
MILLER, Lala B. 23
MILLER, Lonnie D. 17
MILLER, Lonnie Daniel...........17
MILLER, Margaret A. 17
MILLER, Mary C. 16
MILLER, Ora Ozzella.............17
MILLER, Pamlia Ann..............37
MILLER, W.B. 17
MILLER, W.J. 16
MILLER, William Loyd............17
MINCEY, Ben Frank 55
MINCEY, Margie Ruth 55
MINCEY, Martha Jones 55
MINCEY, Mary Sue 55
MINCY, B.A. 55
MIZE, Larry Elton 61
MOBLEY, Henry W. 72
MOBLEY, Iva L. 72
MOBLEY, Lucy J. 71
MOBLEY, Nancy C. 72
MOBLEY, Williams H. 72
MOORE, Betsey J. 40
MOORE, Gertrude H. 74
MOORE, James W. 40
MOORE, Matt 74
MOORE, Matt, Dr. 74
MOORE, Sarah O. 74
MOORE, Sarah Oliver 74
MORTON, William H. 60
MURRAY, John I. 40
MURRAY, Martha L. Carr..........81
MURRAY, Minnie D. 40
MURRAY, Obed W. 81
MURRAY, P.S. 40
MURRAY, S.H. 40

MURRAY, Sarah M. 40
MURRAY, Stephen H. 40

N

NICHOLSON, Charlie M. 23
NICHOLSON, Georgia B. 23
NICHOLSON, Kater Morris.........24
NORRIS, Daniel A. 39
NORRIS, Ethelyn B. 39
NUNN, Henry C. 28
NUNN, John W. 28
NUNN, Lillie C. 31
NUNN, Mary E. 28
NUNN, Mary Elizabeth 28
NUNN, W.F. 28
NUNN, William F. 28
NUNN, Wm. F. 28

O

O'DANIEL, James 77
O'DANIEL, Margaret Anne Grady ..77
O'DANIEL, Rolulus 77
OUTLAW, A.G. 25
OUTLAW, Alexander 28
OUTLAW, Alfred James............26
OUTLAW, Alma Irene...............4
OUTLAW, Alonzo G. 25
OUTLAW, Alpha Mae................26
OUTLAW, Alton (Abbie) 27
OUTLAW, Andrew J. 21
OUTLAW, Annie Collier Whitfield.29
OUTLAW, Annie E...................4
OUTLAW, Annie W. 29
OUTLAW, Arthur...................21
OUTLAW, B. 54
OUTLAW, B.H. 4
OUTLAW, B.T. 28
OUTLAW, Benjamin Haywood.........5
OUTLAW, Bessie C. 22
OUTLAW, Bettie H. 27
OUTLAW, Bettie Harper 27
OUTLAW, Betty Cobb..............29
OUTLAW, Beulah W. 12
OUTLAW, Billy....................80
OUTLAW, Bryant T. 28
OUTLAW, Burtie Herring..........54
OUTLAW, Charity 28
OUTLAW, Charlie D. 22
OUTLAW, Charlotte...............26
OUTLAW, Clara F. 26
OUTLAW, Clarence.................22
OUTLAW, Claudie H. 26

OUTLAW, Cleveland...............18
OUTLAW, D.J. 22,26
OUTLAW, Daisy...................29
OUTLAW, Decie H. 19
OUTLAW, Donald Erie............25
OUTLAW, Donnie.................25
OUTLAW, Dora Blizzard..........18
OUTLAW, Edward 28
OUTLAW, Elizabeth 28
OUTLAW, Elizabeth Grady 28
OUTLAW, Elizabeth J. 27
OUTLAW, Ella Heath.............22
OUTLAW, Emma.................4,22
OUTLAW, Emma D.................22
OUTLAW, Emma M..................4
OUTLAW, F.C....................18
OUTLAW, Francis................26
OUTLAW, Fred...................26
OUTLAW, G. Frank................2
OUTLAW, George L...............26
OUTLAW, George W...............26
OUTLAW, Georgia G..............28
OUTLAW, Grace Smith............29
OUTLAW, H. A. 27
OUTLAW, Henrettia Summerlin.....18
OUTLAW, Henry A. 27
OUTLAW, Herman.................19
OUTLAW, Hettie.................22
OUTLAW, Holand W...............21
OUTLAW, I. V. 27
OUTLAW, Infant.................26
OUTLAW, Infant dau. 25
OUTLAW, Infant son..........22,54
OUTLAW, Infant twin son.........4
OUTLAW, Isaac Vance 27
OUTLAW, J.H. 25,26
OUTLAW, J.J. 21
OUTLAW, J.W., Sr. 22
OUTLAW, Jack...................29
OUTLAW, James B. 28
OUTLAW, James Bryant...........28
OUTLAW, James, Capt............28
OUTLAW, James Clifton..........18
OUTLAW, James, Jr. 28
OUTLAW, James Romie............28
OUTLAW, Jeff...................29
OUTLAW, Joe....................22
OUTLAW, John...................28
OUTLAW, John E.................26
OUTLAW, John Henry.............26
OUTLAW, Johnnie W..............20
OUTLAW, Joseph.................22
OUTLAW, Joseph Edward...........4
OUTLAW, Joseph Ida.............25

OUTLAW, Katie..................25
OUTLAW, Katie O. 25
OUTLAW, L.W. 26
OUTLAW, Lannie D. 26
OUTLAW, Larry James............4
OUTLAW, Laure Heath............21
OUTLAW, Lawton..................4
OUTLAW, Lena Bell..............25
OUTLAW, Leon A. 12
OUTLAW, Leon D.................19
OUTLAW, Leon _?_, Jr. 19
OUTLAW, Leslie..................4
OUTLAW, Lester, Mr. & Mrs. 20
OUTLAW, Lewis..................27
OUTLAW, Lewis..................28
OUTLAW, Lina...................80
OUTLAW, Lossie I. 28
OUTLAW, Lucille Jones..........21
OUTLAW, Lucy....................4
OUTLAW, Lucy Gallagher..........5
OUTLAW, Luther.................26
OUTLAW, Martha Harrell.........21
OUTLAW, Mary...................28
OUTLAW, Mary Ann...............20
OUTLAW, Mary E.................26
OUTLAW, Mathew Lafayette.......25
OUTLAW, Maud...................27
OUTLAW, Mettie J................2
OUTLAW, Milton 27
OUTLAW, Mordecai................4
OUTLAW, N. B. 29
OUTLAW, Nancy 28
OUTLAW, Nathalie Elizabeth.....29
OUTLAW, Needham B..............29
OUTLAW, Needham Bryan..........29
OUTLAW, Needham F..............47
OUTLAW, Nettie Herring.........21
OUTLAW, Noah...................26
OUTLAW, Norman DeLeon..........22
OUTLAW, O.E. 26
OUTLAW, Patience 28
OUTLAW, Paul...................25
OUTLAW, Penelope...............29
OUTLAW, Penelope O.............29
OUTLAW, Rachel E. "Betty".......47
OUTLAW, Ralph W................27
OUTLAW, Randolph J. 27
OUTLAW, Ray L..................21
OUTLAW, Richard H..............29
OUTLAW, Richard Harding........29
OUTLAW, Samuel.................22
OUTLAW, Selma Jane..............4
OUTLAW, Smithy.................29
OUTLAW, Susan A. Summerlin.....22

OUTLAW, Trudie M. 20
OUTLAW, Viola H.................4
OUTLAW, W. 54
OUTLAW, William 28
OUTLAW, William L. 22
OUTLAW, Willie.................54
OUTLAW, Willie I...............21
OUTLAW, Wineferd............25,26
OUTLAW, Wineferd Potter........26

P

PAGE, John A. 23
PARKER, Annie Garner...........21
PARKER, Celia..................21
PARKER, Joe Berry..............21
PARKER, Mathew.................21
PARKER, Mattie Sue 61
PARKER, Senas..................21
PARKER, Sula...................21
PARROTT, Angela D., infant.......5
PATE, Carlyle Franklin..........14
PATE, Emma Louis 65
PATE, John Burton 65
PATE, John Willard 65
PATE, Larry Joe................14
PATE, Ruby Lee Brogden.........14
PATE, Willard 65
PEARCE, Hughey A. 68
PEARCE, Lue Eliza..............68
PEARSELL, Eugene...............24
PEELE, Rachel J. 47
PEELE, S.W. 47
PHILLIPS, Ebby.................46
PHILLIPS, Girtie...............46
PHILLIPS, J.J..................46
PHILLIPS, M.J..................46
PHILLIPS, Mary A...............46
PHILLIPS, Rostion..............46
PHIPPS, [M]elly C. 81
PHIPPS, Milly 81
PHIPPS, William H..............81
PHIPPS, Wm. P..................81
PICKETT, Beulah................32
PICKETT, Hester vii,58
PICKETT, Maxey A. 72
PICKETT, William vii,58
PIERCE, Hannah Harrette........20
PIERCE, Nancy Susan............20
PIERCE, Sampson................20
POTTER, Addie Summerlin........20
POTTER, Paul...................20
POTTER, Robert C. 20
POTTER, Robert T. 20

POWELL, Hettie M. Sutton Barbrey38
POYTHRESS, Laura B. 53
POYTHRESS, Richard P. 53
PRICE, Essie Mae................5
PRICE, Freddie J. 66
PRICE, J.T. 42
PRICE, John T. 42
PRICE, Lula....................42
PRICE, Marion McDonald..........3
Price, Mary Bell 66
PRICE, Wilbert W...............5
PRIDGEN, Ethel.................44
PRIDGEN, John.................44
PRIDGEN, John William........43
PRIDGEN, Nettie R. 44
PRIDGEN, Robert Morris........44

Q

QUINN, Geo. D. 9
QUINN, Herman, Mr. & Mrs. 20
QUINN, Infant son...........20,47
QUINN, Infant twin daus. 47
QUINN, Jesse..................47
QUINN, Jesse J. 13
QUINN, Johnnie Allen..........29
QUINN, Lucy...................47
QUINN, Mary R. 13
QUINN, Pearl..................47
QUINN, Susan..................46
QUINN, W.I. 47
QUINN, Wm. I. 46

R

RACKLEY, Dora V. Robinson.......35
RACKLEY, F.P. 35
RACKLEY, Franklin P. 35
RACKLEY, J.A. 35
RACKLEY, J.C. 35
RACKLEY, John C. 35
RACKLEY, Z.J. 35
RACKLEY, Zilpha J. 35
RAYNOR, Dave William..........32
RAYNOR, L.C. 34
RAYNOR, Lewis C. 34
RAYNOR, Mary.................34
RAYNOR, Rachel F. 34
REGISTER, Cathrine E. 40
REGISTER, E.G. 40
REGISTER, Lela...............40
REGISTER, Olivia.............53
RHODES, Ann..................16
RHODES, James T. vii,16

RHODES, John F. 16
RHODES, Joseph T. 16
RHODES, Maria................16
RHODES, Maria S. 16
RHODES, Mary P. 16
RHODES, Mary..............vii,16
RHODES, Rachel..............16
RHODES, Temperance...........16
RITTER, Charity C. 77
RITTER, Ida 77
RITTER, Ida Pearl 77
ROBERTS, Annie...............13
ROBERTS, B.C. 13
ROBERTS, Bertice Carl Sr. 13
ROBERTS, Henry..............13
ROBERTS, Infant dau. 13
ROBERTS, Jerry Lee...........13
ROBERTS, Margaret............13
ROBERTS, Melissa West........13
ROBERTS, Nancy Katherine.....13
ROBERTS, Ned................13
ROBINSON, Henry S. 26
ROBINSON, Juanita............49
ROBINSON, Robert.............49
RODGERS, Callie Mae..........3
RODGERS, Carl................3
RODGERS, Chancey.............18
RODGERS, George..............18
RODGERS, Georgia.............18
RODGERS, Georgiana...........18
RODGERS, Giles 63
RODGERS, Jimmie 63
RODGERS, Lula................18
RODGERS, Paul................3
ROGERS, Alphina..............3
ROGERS, Alphina Outlaw.......3
ROGERS, (cemetery)...........79
ROGERS, Clarkey..............24
ROGERS, Frank 63
ROGERS, Giles 63
ROGERS, Hattie 63
ROGERS, Infant twins.........18
ROGERS, Julia................18
ROGERS, Luke.................18
ROGERS, Margaret 63
ROGERS, Nancy 63
ROGERS, Pina.................3
ROGERS, Robert L. 20
ROGERS, Ruth O. 20
ROGERS, Thad.................3
ROGERS, Tony Lee 63
ROGERS, Yancy 63
ROUSE, Dollie Wells 79
ROUSE, H.F. 79

ROUSE, Infant son...........46,79
ROUSE, Infants...............79
ROUSE, Isabel 79
ROUSE, J.Q. 46
ROUSE, James 79
ROUSE, James, Mr. & Mrs. 79
ROUSE, Joe 79
ROUSE, Joe, Sr. 79
ROUSE, Joseph S. 79
ROUSE, Julia.................46
ROUSE, Julia Quinn...........46
ROUSE, M.D. 79
ROUSE, Reba Lue..............46
ROUSE, Sarah A. Farrier 79
ROUSE, W.C. 46
ROYALL, A.P. 13
ROYALL, Arthur P. 13
ROYALL, Elizabeth Roberts....13
ROYALL, Robert W. 13

S

SASSER, Anna Williams 75
SASSER, D.S. 75
SASSER, J.F. 52
SASSER, Octavia Bennett.......52
SHINE, Elizabeth 16
SHINE, James F. 16
SHINE, Martha R. 16
SIMMONS, Addie L. 31
SIMMONS, D.H. 77
SIMMONS, Mary Carolina 77
SIMMONS, N.D. 31
SIMMONS, Nathan D. 31
SIMMONS, Theodore R. 31
SINGLETON, A.J. 3
SINGLETON, Alsa James........3
SINGLETON, Daisey A..........3
SINGLETON, Rosy..............3
SLOAN, Charles R. 72
SLOAN, Elizabeth 72
SMITH, Allen.................49
SMITH, Chancy................50
SMITH, Chancy I..............8
SMITH, Chancy Ivey...........8
SMITH, Charlie A. 49
SMITH, Infant................8
SMITH, Keneth Ray............8
SMITH, Maggie................8
SMITH, Maggie K..............8
SMITH, Margret May...........8
SMITH, Mary S. 49
SMITH, Polly.................50
SMITH, Susan E. Adkinson.....24

SMITH, Thomas....................24
SMITH, Troy......................49
SMITH, Willie.....................8
SOUTHERLAND, Abbie W. 23
SOUTHERLAND, Annie Best........23
SOUTHERLAND, Annie M. 23
SOUTHERLAND, C.C. 23
SOUTHERLAND, C.E. 22
SOUTHERLAND, Cannie E. Grady....22
SOUTHERLAND, Cecil Garland.....23
SOUTHERLAND, Charles Clay......23
SOUTHERLAND, E.B. 23
SOUTHERLAND, E.T. 51
SOUTHERLAND, Flora Bell........22
SOUTHERLAND, H.D. 23
SOUTHERLAND, Henry............23
SOUTHERLAND, Infant...........79
SOUTHERLAND, Infant dau. 22
SOUTHERLAND, Infant son......22,23
SOUTHERLAND, J.D. 79
SOUTHERLAND, J.N. 51
SOUTHERLAND, John R. 22
SOUTHERLAND, L.G. 22
SOUTHERLAND, Leonard G. 22
SOUTHERLAND, Mary Wells........79
SOUTHERLAND, Ren V. 23
SOUTHERLAND, Ruby P. 22
SOUTHERLAND, Ruth Mildred......23
SOUTHERLAND, Soohronie Winders..22
SOUTHERLAND, Stella E. 51
SOUTHERLAND, Wren.............23
STANFORD, Samuel, Rev. vii,44
STANFORD, Scott.................44
STORASKA, Frederick, Mr. & Mrs. 23
STORASKA, Infant son............23
STROUD, Albert.............30,48
STROUD, Annie..............48,49
STROUD, Annie S. 49
STROUD, Annie T. 48
STROUD, Ashley................48
STROUD, baby boy..............48
STROUD, baby girl.............48
STROUD, Barney................30
STROUD, Benjamin F. 30
STROUD, Bertie Cora...........48
STROUD, Betty Jean............48
STROUD, C. Raymond............49
STROUD, Carrie G. 30
STROUD, Charlie...............48
STROUD, Charlotte.............49
STROUD, Charlotte E. 49
STROUD, Clyde.................30
STROUD, Donnie................48
STROUD, Doris M. 30

STROUD, Edna..................29
STROUD, Effie Lee.............48
STROUD, Egbert................30
STROUD, Elcie A. 48
STROUD, Esther P. 30
STROUD, Esther Pease..........30
STROUD, Fannie M. 30
STROUD, Glenn M. 30
STROUD, Gordon................48
STROUD, Hazel Estell..........49
STROUD, Hugh..................30
STROUD, I.T. 30
STROUD, Ida W. 30
STROUD, Infant................48
STROUD, Infant son............30
STROUD, Isaac.................30
STROUD, Isaac Thomas, Rev. 30
STROUD, Jagold................48
STROUD, Jagold Jr. 48
STROUD, Jeremiah..............30
STROUD, Jobe..................49
STROUD, John E. 31
STROUD, Lannie................49
STROUD, Lannie C. 47
STROUD, Leslie................48
STROUD, Leslie Jr. 48
STROUD, Lyda S. 30
STROUD, Mannie................30
STROUD, Mannie P. 30
STROUD, Marie.................30
STROUD, Marie Young...........30
STROUD, Mary..................48
STROUD, Mary M. 31
STROUD, Mattie................48
STROUD, Moten.................49
STROUD, Moten Harold..........48
STROUD, Nancy W. 48
STROUD, Needham...............29
STROUD, Nellie................48
STROUD, Nellie Lee............48
STROUD, Nelma F. 48
STROUD, Oscar.................49
STROUD, Owen...............30,48
STROUD, Patsy Jewel...........29
STROUD, Raymond...............49
STROUD, Sallie R. 48
STROUD, _?_rl.................48
STROUD, Thurman...............30
STROWD?, Croom................51
STROWD?, Susan W. 51
SULLIVAN, Carolyn Faye 61
SULLIVAN, George Washington......5
SULLIVAN, Georgia................5
SULLIVAN, Georgia Taylor.........5

SULLIVAN, H.......................5
SULLIVAN, Henry...................4
SULLIVAN, Hoyt Jackson............5
SULLIVAN, John Henry..............5
SULLIVAN, William 61
SUMMERLIN, Ada J. 19
SUMMERLIN, Addie Jones 66
SUMMERLIN, Alonzo Daniel.........19
SUMMERLIN, Benjamin P. 19
SUMMERLIN, Bessie................11
SUMMERLIN, Carrie J. Sutton......38
SUMMERLIN, Dealie R. 65
SUMMERLIN, Debbie Jean...........65
SUMMERLIN, E. J. 65
SUMMERLIN, Ebbert 65
SUMMERLIN, Edgar J. 65
SUMMERLIN, Edieth Whitfield.....41
SUMMERLIN, Edna M. 65
SUMMERLIN, Effie.................11
SUMMERLIN, Eliza.................12
SUMMERLIN, Eliza E. 12
SUMMERLIN, Emma D. 66
SUMMERLIN, Floyd 18,65
SUMMERLIN, G.L. 20
SUMMERLIN, George Lawton.........20
SUMMERLIN, Haywood................1
SUMMERLIN, Hepsie Jones...........1
SUMMERLIN, Herbert J. 66
SUMMERLIN, Infant dau.............1
SUMMERLIN, Infant son.........3,20
SUMMERLIN, Ira Jr.................1
SUMMERLIN, Ira Randolph...........1
SUMMERLIN, Ivey...................3
SUMMERLIN, J.D. 41
SUMMERLIN, J.L. 19
SUMMERLIN, J.M. 12
SUMMERLIN, Jim...................11
SUMMERLIN, John D. 19
SUMMERLIN, John Daniel...........18
SUMMERLIN, John H. 65
SUMMERLIN, John L. 65
SUMMERLIN, John M. 12
SUMMERLIN, Kate..................20
SUMMERLIN, Kate Agnes Williams..20
SUMMERLIN, Lacy 65
SUMMERLIN, Lannie Ezzell 66
SUMMERLIN, Lewis J. 66
SUMMERLIN, Lucy 65
SUMMERLIN, Lucy L. 65
SUMMERLIN, M.O. 38
SUMMERLIN, Mack..................11
SUMMERLIN, Maggie K. 19
SUMMERLIN, Margaret..............19
SUMMERLIN, Margaret Parker......19

SUMMERLIN, Mary S. 65
SUMMERLIN, McCoy Stephen.......20
SUMMERLIN, Minnie..............1
SUMMERLIN, Minnie Carter........1
SUMMERLIN, Minnie M............1
SUMMERLIN, Minnie W. 20
SUMMERLIN, Nancy 65
SUMMERLIN, Nannie Lou Grady.....20
SUMMERLIN, Nora...............3
SUMMERLIN, Nora L.............3
SUMMERLIN, Norman.............11
SUMMERLIN, Robert Lee.........19
SUMMERLIN, Rodolph.............1
SUMMERLIN, Sallie E. 12
SUMMERLIN, Samuel Paul.........19
SUMMERLIN, W.C. 20
SUMMERLIN, Zilphia Ann.........18
SUTTON, Anna Kathrine.........37
SUTTON, Ben...................6
SUTTON, Chellis E. 41
SUTTON, Clarence 56
SUTTON, Cora..................38
SUTTON, Daniel Kirby..........27
SUTTON, Daniel Roscoe.........5
SUTTON, E.B. 38
SUTTON, E.J. 38
SUTTON, Edward B. 38
SUTTON, Elva Jane.............38
SUTTON, Emma L. 38
SUTTON, F.L. 38
SUTTON, Fannie Hood...........38
SUTTON, Fonnie................30
SUTTON, Frances Olivia........38
SUTTON, Geo. T. 38
SUTTON, Giles.................54
SUTTON, Helen.................37
SUTTON, Henry.................31
SUTTON, Ida L. 15
SUTTON, Infant dau. 26
SUTTON, Infant son........5,26,38
SUTTON, Ivey..................26
SUTTON, Ivey B. 26
SUTTON, J.D. 41
SUTTON, J.H. 26
SUTTON, J. Harvey.............52
SUTTON, Jessie................5
SUTTON, Kittie..............30,31
SUTTON, Kittie S..............30
SUTTON, Lena..................26
SUTTON, Lewis M. 52
SUTTON, Lillian Adell 27
SUTTON, Lucy L. 38
SUTTON, M. 52
SUTTON, M.H. 15,27,37

SUTTON, Major W. 27
SUTTON, Margaret C. Futtrell....52
SUTTON, Nellie................5
SUTTON, Nellie W. 5
SUTTON, O.W. 38
SUTTON, O.W., Jr. 38
SUTTON, Oswin W. 38
SUTTON, Patience............26,27
SUTTON, Patience E. 26
SUTTON, Pearl C. 56
SUTTON, Pearl Wilkins..........6
SUTTON, Sara Carrie...........38
SUTTON, T.H. 26,27
SUTTON, T.W. 52
SUTTON, T.W., Jr. 52
SUTTON, Thomas A. 26
SUTTON, Thomas H. 27
SUTTON, Thomas William........52
SUTTON, W.I. 30,31
SUTTON, William E. 6
SUTTON, William I. 30
SUTTON, William Oswin.........38
SUTTON, Wm. Ben...............52
SWINSON, Alice Roosevelt......17
SWINSON, Alonza E. 72
SWINSON, Andrew T. 18
SWINSON, Ben..................18
SWINSON, Betty Gale...........13
SWINSON, Bobby G. 13
SWINSON, C.H. 18
SWINSON, Callie Brock.........18
SWINSON, (cemetery)...........79
SWINSON, Charlie E. 72
SWINSON, Charlie H. 18
SWINSON, Charlotte............17
SWINSON, Cyrus Thompson.......17
SWINSON, Daniel...............17
SWINSON, Frances W. 18
SWINSON, Frank 72
SWINSON, George Marcus........17
SWINSON, Gurtrude.............17
SWINSON, Henry................17
SWINSON, James A. 13
SWINSON, James Auston.........43
SWINSON, James G. 72
SWINSON, Jesse.........vii,17,43
SWINSON, JoAnn................13
SWINSON, Joe..................18
SWINSON, John.................18
SWINSON, Julia A. 72
SWINSON, Levi C. 72
SWINSON, Lola.................17
SWINSON, Margarette Lee.......18
SWINSON, Mary E. 18

SWINSON, Mary E. Hardy.........18
SWINSON, Minnie...............18
SWINSON, Myrtle Ann Jones......18
SWINSON, Nancy............vii,43
SWINSON, Richard R. 72
SWINSON, Rossie W. 13
SWINSON, Susan................18
SWINSON, William R. 72

T

TAYLOR, Baby..................8
TAYLOR, Beadie...............9
TAYLOR, Ben..................9
TAYLOR, Ben Frank............9
TAYLOR, Budd.................8
TAYLOR, Cammie Rogers........3
TAYLOR, Carrie...............8
TAYLOR, Charlotte Elizabeth 63
TAYLOR, Elizabeth............52
TAYLOR, Gurney...............8
TAYLOR, Henry James..........3
TAYLOR, Infant son..........8,9
TAYLOR, Isham U. 52
TAYLOR, J.H. 50
TAYLOR, James................8
TAYLOR, James R. 9
TAYLOR, Jesse K. 52
TAYLOR, Johnny C. 51
TAYLOR, L.C. Rev. 63
TAYLOR, Mattie...............9
TAYLOR, Paul.................8
TAYLOR, Pearcy Jane..........12
TAYLOR, Polly................8
TAYLOR, Will.................8
TAYLOR, William..............54
TEACHEY, Billy...............40
TEACHEY, Infant dau. 40
TEACHEY, Infant son..........40
TEACHEY, Leona M. 40
THIGPEN, A.L. 4
THIGPEN, Alex................5
THIGPEN, Infant son..........4
THIGPEN, J.C. 4
THIGPEN, Jessie O. 5
THOMAS, Charlie..............35
THOMAS, Margaret C. 35
THOMPSON, J.T. 53
THOMPSON, Jennie.............53
THOMPSON, Virginia...........53
THORNTON, J.D. 15
THORNTON, Polly L. 15
TILLMAN, Alec................80
TILLMAN, Bessie Vinson.......80

TILLMAN, John.................80
TILLMAN, Lalar...............80
TILLMAN, Lula................80
TILLMAN, [Mary?] Sutton Outlaw..80
TILLMAN, Norman..............80
TORRANS, Samuel C. 34
TORRANS, Thomas K. 34
TURNER, Alfred...............11
TURNER, D.J. 42
TURNER, Dolly Jane Elizabeth....49
TURNER, Durwood..............49
TURNER, Esther Mae T. 11
TURNER, Eva..................11
TURNER, Garland Odell........11
TURNER, James Perry..........11
TURNER, Lola Garner..........42
TURNER, Martin...............49
TURNER, Mollie...............49
TURNER, Pearl J. 66
TURNER, Robert Earl..........49
TURNER, Roland O. 66
TYNDALL, A.E. 46
TYNDALL, Emma................46
TYNDALL, Infant..............46
TYNDALL, Mabel Carter 59

U

UNDERHILL, Annie F. 14
UNDERHILL, Frances...........14
UNDERHILL, G.W. 14
UNDERHILL, George W. 14
UNDERHILL, J.W. 14
UNDERHILL, Littie A. 14

V

VERNON, E. L. 66
VERNON, Edwin L. 66
VERNON, Henry Preston 65
VERNON, M. K. 66
VERNON, Maude A. 66
VERNON, Melvin Gray 66

W

WALKER, Jesse................43
WALKER, Nancy................43
WARD, Richard O. 13
WASHINGTON, Mary Ann.........51
WASHINGTON, Richard..........51
WATERS, Carey D. 3
WATERS, Clara B. 3
WATERS, Clara Bell...........3

WATERS, Dora G. 60
WATERS, G.D. 3
WATERS, George D. 3
WATERS, M.J. 53
WATERS, Matilda P. 53
WATERS, Mildred..............3
WATKINS, E. 46
WATKINS, Kate 71
WATKINS, W.R. 46
WATKINS, Windol R. 46
WEEKS, Arthur 75
WEEKS, Sarah A. 75
WELLS, Mac 79
WELLS, Mrs. 79
WELLS, R.D. 79
WELLS, Raymond...............79
WEST, Hollan A. 49
WESTBROOK, Jessie 64
WESTBROOK, Jessie Jr. 64
WESTBROOK, Mollie 64
WHALEY, Betty Alberta........32
WHALEY, Empie J. 32
WHALEY, Hazel Glenn..........32
WHALEY, Ida Halso............32
WHALEY, J.R. 32
WHALEY, James Franklin.......32
WHALEY, James R. 32
WHALEY, Martha E. 32
WHITE, Betty Lynn............23
WHITFIELD, Adline 27
WHITFIELD, B.H. 41
WHITFIELD, Dan...............24
WHITFIELD, Fannie Adell......47
WHITFIELD, Ina 27
WHITFIELD, J.P. 24
WHITFIELD, Jasper 27
WHITFIELD, Johnie............47
WHITFIELD, L.H. 47
WHITFIELD, Lemuel H. 47
WHITFIELD, Likie 27
WHITFIELD, Lucy Outlaw.......47
WHITFIELD, W. J. 27
WHITLEY, William A. 36
WHITMAN, Barney W. 41
WHITMAN, Betsey..............12
WHITMAN, Doney H. 41
WHITMAN, G.H. 12
WHITMAN, George H. 12
WHITMAN, Infant son..........12
WHITMAN, Nancy Susan.........41
WHITMAN, Nora................12
WHITMAN, Nora E. 12
WHITMAN, Riley...............12
WHITMAN, Wright..............41

WILEY, Albert M. 61
WILEY, Myrtle J. 61
WILKINS, B. Frank 56
WILKINS, Ben Frank 56
WILKINS, Bradley 56
WILKINS, Cassie Dail 56
WILKINS, Charley 55
WILKINS, Emmett 56
WILKINS, Frank 56
WILKINS, Frank 56
WILKINS, Franklin D. 56
WILKINS, H. [T.] 56
WILKINS, Infant 56
WILKINS, Louvenia 56
WILKINS, Mary Ellen 56
WILKINS, Patsy 56
WILKINS, Pearl 56
WILKINS, Sarah 55
WILKINS, Vivie 56
WILKINS, Vivie H. 56
WILLIAMS, Anna Davis.........21
WILLIAMS, B. W. 75
WILLIAMS, Baby...............32
WILLIAMS, Carrie Herring.....45
WILLIAMS, D.W. 21
WILLIAMS, Eddie Bowden 75
WILLIAMS, Electra Lestina ...73
WILLIAMS, Eliza 82
WILLIAMS, Elizabeth A. 73
WILLIAMS, Elizabeth E. 73
WILLIAMS, Elizabeth Ezzell ..73
WILLIAMS, Ellen E. 73
WILLIAMS, Fannie.............6
WILLIAMS, Fedorah Mrs. 82
WILLIAMS, Florence E. 68
WILLIAMS, H. Julia Lanier....68
WILLIAMS, H. W. 82
WILLIAMS, Harper........vii,82
WILLIAMS, Hettie H. 67
WILLIAMS, Infant.............43
WILLIAMS, Infant dau. 69,82
WILLIAMS, J.B. 45
WILLIAMS, J. F. 73
WILLIAMS, J. K. 73
WILLIAMS, J.R. 69
WILLIAMS, James 82
WILLIAMS, James K. 73
WILLIAMS, James M. 82
WILLIAMS, Jas. Boney.........45
WILLIAMS, Jas. M. 82
WILLIAMS, Jerry A. 67
WILLIAMS, Jessie W. 67
WILLIAMS, John E. 67,82
WILLIAMS, John Wesley........68

WILLIAMS, Lamuel Holt..........68
WILLIAMS, Lamuel...........vii,68
WILLIAMS, Lesley................6
WILLIAMS, Letha...............69
WILLIAMS, Linster.............69
WILLIAMS, Major Ellis..........69
WILLIAMS, Martha...............82
WILLIAMS, Martha L. 75
WILLIAMS, Martha Lorenza 75
WILLIAMS, Martha Mrs. 81
WILLIAMS, Mary C. 68
WILLIAMS, Mary Helen 73
WILLIAMS, Mollie Louise 75
WILLIAMS, Motsey 75
WILLIAMS, Nancy Jane...........67
WILLIAMS, Perry N. 68
WILLIAMS, Precilla.............32
WILLIAMS, Priscilla............69
WILLIAMS, Redin Croton 75
WILLIAMS, Sallie..............68
WILLIAMS, Sallie Earnesteen......6
WILLIAMS, Sarah B. 67
WILLIAMS, (wife of Jas. M.) 82
WILLIAMS, William H. 81
WILLIAMSON, Pitt 57
WINDERS, Luther...............22
WINDERS, Myrtie S. 65
WINDERS, Sarah................22
WINDERS, Walter Lee...........22
WOOD, Joy.......................32
WOOD, Mary B. 32
WOOD, Sarah Magaline...........32
WOODARD, Infant dau. 46
WOODARD, L.B. 46
WOODARD, W.R. 46
WOODARD, Warren R., Jr.,"Buddy".46
WRIGHT, Charity vii,74
WRIGHT, Eliza.............vii,51
WRIGHT, James vii,74
WRIGHT, John Beck vii,74
WRIGHT, John D. 51
WRIGHT, Thomas B. 51
WRIGHT, Thomas.............vii,51